College Casualties

Twelve Competencies to Avoid
Becoming One

Dr. Lourdes Ferrer

Dr. Lourdes Ferrer

Title: College Casualties

Subtitle: Twelve Competencies to Avoid Becoming One

Author: Dr. Lourdes Ferrer

This book presents the twelve competencies that students must demonstrate to avoid becoming one more college casualty. College casualties is defined by Dr. Ferrer as students who drop out of one college, earn degrees that are not in demand or graduate college with unsurmountable amounts of debts.

ISBN-10: 1508856982

ISBN-13:978-1508856986

DEDICATION

I dedicate this book to my husband, Sylvester Allen Jr. For years, he has insisted that I write a book for high school students. In his own words, "You have written books for teachers and parents. What about the kids? Don't you think they also need to know how to excel in school?" He was my motivation and sounding board for the ideas presented in this book.

> *Sylvester, thank you for the companionship and collaboration that you provided me with throughout my journey of reaching out and helping high school students achieve greater academic success.*

RECOGNITIONS

The first person I must recognize is Ms. Maria Lozano, the Director of the English as a Second Language and Bilingual Education Department in School District 129. She contracted my services years ago to work with the Hispanic community in the city of West Aurora, Illinois. It was under her leadership that I was able to help so many families successfully navigate the American Education System. Maria provided me with the platform I needed to be creative and the opportunity to touch so many lives.

Maria, I will always remember you as a highly qualified and caring professional. You are the best boss ever. I love you sister!

I must also recognize the group of students from West Aurora High School who participated in the 2013-14, Grooming for Excellence Student Leadership Academy. They inspired me to spend time and energy thinking about the challenges students face in their pursuit of a quality education. These students, all high achievers, studied and reacted to the twelve competencies presented in this book.

Some of them went a step further – they accepted the challenge of writing the essays that are included in this book. These students were - Alexis Davila, Armando J. Davila, Christian Ramirez, Christopher Rodriguez, David Ballines, Evelyn Ganchuz, Hesiquio Ballines, Karina Callegos, Irving Espinoza, Jimena Moreno, Melissa Medellin, Nicolas Barrios and Rodolfo Lozano Jr.

My dear students, I will never forget the time we spent together. Students like you inspire educators like me to continue with our mission to provide a quality education to all children. To you I say, "You have been groomed for excellence! Never forget that a quality education is the door to a quality life."

Dr. Lourdes Ferrer

SPECIAL THANKS

I want to thank the parents of the students who not only participated in the *Grooming for Excellence Student Leadership Academy* but also wrote the essays included in this book. These dedicated parents provided the kind of motivation and support their kids needed to meet with me on numerous Saturday mornings and spend time and energy writing the essays.

Special thanks to Mr. Jose Torres, the professional photographer who took the students' picture on the back cover of this book. Jose not only did not charge us for his excellent work but also did so with great care, kindness and love.

I also want to express thanks to Mr. David Zimmerman, a dedicated teacher, who spent numerous hours editing the essays that students wrote and are included in this book. He kindly volunteered to do this time-consuming work and did so with an admirable enthusiasm and care for the kids.

CONTENTS

STUDENT ESSAYS

INTRODUCTION

Hi, I am Dr. Lourdes. If you are reading this introduction is because you are considering reading this book. You might be a parent, a high school student or a teacher curious about, "How in the world a student who enrolls in college becomes a casualty?"

Baby boomers like me, more than any other generation are aware of how much the world has changed. Technology has transformed the way we live our lives. As a result, students are now required to learn rigorous content, at earlier grades and at a "microwave" rather than conventional oven speed. Because 80% of the fastest-growing jobs now require some sort of post-secondary education, a high school diploma alone no longer leads to high-in-demand and high-paying careers. Aware of this reality, in record numbers, high school graduates are enrolling in college. A veteran high school teacher said to me the other day,

"Things have changed so much in my school. Twenty years ago, few students sought receiving a college education; and they were usually the high achievers,

considered by teachers as college-bound kids. Today, every kid is planning to go to college, even the ones who show little interest in their education."

As a nation, we are now facing a new and unprecedented challenge - too many of our high school graduates are sadly becoming, what we call in this book - *college casualties*. A significant number of students who enroll in college never graduate and the few, who complete their college education, are graduating with degrees that are not in demand and/or with surmountable amounts of debts.

This is why I decided to spend the past three years mining into this challenge in search for understanding. I wanted to know the reasons behind students dropping out of college, earning degrees that lead to unemployment or underemployment or getting into debts that are impossible to pay. I also wanted to know what educational leaders could do to minimize or eliminate the number of students who become college casualties. My dear reader, this is what this book is all about.

Knowing that I am almost forty years older than a regular high school student is I decided to invite my daughter Deborah Ferrer to assist me in the process of writing this book. My decades of experience working with students, parents and teachers combined with Deborah's youth and recent college experiences could provide readers like you the awareness, insights and strategies that high school students need to graduate college, debt-free and with degrees that lead to high-in-demand careers. Anyone who reads this book can benefit by learning how a high school student can avoid paths that lead to academic failure, unemployment and financial burden.

Dr. Lourdes Ferrer

PROLOGUE

Let me tell you a story about my best friend, Rick, who is the most intelligent person I have ever met in my entire life. I met him in church almost 20 years ago, when I was a doctoral student at Florida Atlantic University. I was born and raised in Puerto Rico, and spent much of my adult life in Central America, so my English language and computer skills were very limited. Writing an essay, creating a Power Point presentation and even navigating the Internet were overwhelming challenges. He was the only person I could turn to for help. He became my mentor and academic coach.

What took me completely by surprise was that Rick was a college dropout. As smart as he was, he did not even have a college degree. At that time, I did not believe that was possible. Why did he quit? In his own words, "When I started college, I did not know what I was getting myself into." Rick was raised in a strong Christian environment, in a small town in the state of Michigan. No one in his family had ever attended college and at that time, the only people that he knew who had a college degree were teachers, people in the medical field and ministers. After graduating high school he enrolled at the Michigan State University, which was two hours away from home, just to be with his best friend and avoid being alone. He was academically ready to go to college but totally unprepared to navigate a post-secondary academic world. Rick was counselled to become a Chemical Engineer. It made sense because he was very good in math and science. According to Rick, "It was a fit for my ability but not my personality. I didn't know how to choose a major that fit me." Some of his classes had more than a hundred students in them. Some of his professors were difficult to deal with. In his own words, "I had professors that were openly anti-Christian, which made me feel very uncomfortable. Some of the professors barely spoke English, which made difficult subjects even more difficult. "I didn't switch sections because I was raised to be compliant to authority."

His best friend from high school (his roommate at college) began engaging in activities that pulled them apart. That weakened his emotional support. To help support himself he worked 20 hours a week in a permanent part-time job, which required him to stay on campus, when most students were gone for the summer. All these things proved to be too much. Therefore, at the age of twenty, after two years, Rick dropped out of college. He ended up becoming what we call in this book, a college casualty.

It was not until 2005, 33 years later, that he got a wakeup call. Wanting greater flexibility and employment opportunities, he decided to go back to school. In his fifties, he completed a BA in Communication and Organizational Leadership and immediately after that, a MA in Instructional Design eLearning. Today Rick is a successful Instructional Designer and Adjunct Professor at Palm Beach Atlantic University and an Independent Consultant in the Instructional Design field. Reflecting back he states, "Those were thirty-three years of limited job opportunities and reduced earning." Could you imagine Rick's life if he had completed his college degree three decades earlier? This is the reason why I am writing this book. I do not want you to become one more college casualty; that is, one more among millions of American students who enroll in college in pursuit of a career that could open doors to a quality life, and instead end up further away from what they envisioned or hoped to accomplish.

Although there are different ways that students become college casualties, I will address in this book the three causes or reasons that I consider most significant. A student becomes a college casualty when he or she enrolls in college, and for a variety of reasons, never graduates. You probably know people that have never finished their post-secondary education. According to the National Center for Education Statistics, in 2005, only 59% of students enrolled in 4-year institutions completed their bachelor's degree within 6 years. At 2-year degree-granting institutions, the graduation rate was even lower. Only 31% of students who began their pursuit of a certificate or associate's degree graduated within 3 years. This graduation rate was only 20% in 2-year public institutions. One of the greatest challenges that community colleges in the United States face today is not increasing their enrollment but increasing their graduation rate. Some of those students who did not graduate could have done so later on in life, like Rick, but sadly, most do not.

There are numerous reasons why students drop out of college. Some are not academically ready; that is, their reading, writing and math skills are sub-par. This lack of academic proficiency is more evident in our nation's community colleges. A high percent of students are required to take preparatory English and math courses because their standardized test scores disqualifies them to take college level classes. Students who are forced to enroll in prep-courses can get discouraged and dropout. They do not want to spend their time, money and effort in classes that do not count towards a college degree.

Other students drop out because they do not have the financial resources needed to be a full-time student. They must pay, not only their tuition, but also other college-related expenses, such as housing, instructional materials, transportation, and food, just to name a few. They take part-time jobs that consume too much of their time and energy, limiting their time to comply with their student responsibilities. They find it impossible to sustain themselves financially and therefore end up leaving school.

There are also students who simply do not know how to navigate a post-secondary academic world. They are exposed and susceptible to many pitfalls and temptations and the parents are not there to supervise. They are engaged in behaviors that are not conducive to academic success such as alcohol and drug abuse, excessive partying and hanging out with the wrong crowd. These behaviors and activities affect their performance in school and kill their willingness and desire to continue with their education. They lose what it takes to continue in school and drop out.

Although a college degree cannot guarantee a good job, it can significantly increase a person's opportunities to earn a decent living. There are very successful people without a college education. However, these people are outliers, the exception to the rule. The fact is that in today's economy, 80% of the fastest-growing jobs require some kind of post-secondary education. The job opportunities are slim when a young person has only earned a high school diploma.

Dropping out of college not only affects young people's ability to earn a decent living but can also hurt their emotional wellbeing. They are likely to see it as a big loss. Time, energy and resources wasted for nothing! There is no reward or sense of accomplishment in not completing what has been started.

Dropping out of college or not completing an academic program can also affect the way students are perceived by others, especially potential employers. It can be interpreted as lack of commitment, discipline and stability. Employers are likely to overlook people who seem to demonstrate these characteristics.

The second college casualty happens when students earn a degree in careers that are not in demand or pay very little. It is heart breaking to see so many young people in their early twenties unemployed or getting jobs that pay minimum wages, after years of hard academic work. I have been working with students for more than three decades. One thing that has always concerned me is their lack of awareness regarding careers that are in high demand in today's economy. According to the Economic Policy Institute, almost 17% of young college graduates either cannot find a job; are working part-time jobs because they cannot find a full-time; or gave up looking for a job after months of arduous search. For example, they might have degrees in psychology, sociology or business. Although all these degrees are admirable, the number of young adults with these types of degrees outstrips its demand.

Not long ago, I met a young woman in her twenties slowly hauling a huge garbage can through the halls of a county government building. A few minutes later, I saw her in the women restroom. She looked sad and somewhat embarrassed while cleaning the bathroom toilets. After greeting and engaging her in "small talk," naively assuming she lacked a college degree, I asked her, "Have you considered going to college to earn a degree that could open you doors to a better job?" She responded, "I am a college graduate. I have a degree in Psychology but never been able to get a job in my field. My parents will not continue to support me. I have student loans to pay and other bills. So, I desperately needed a job and this was the only one I could get." It totally broke my heart! She was so young and yet so sad. According to the CUNY (City University of New York) report, in the United States, 15% of taxi drivers, 1,000,000 retail clerks, and 115,000 janitors have college degrees. As you can see, not all college degrees lead to high in demand and high-paying careers.

There are several reasons why students pursue careers that are not in demand or that pay very little. One of them is plain ignorance. They simply do not know. They choose careers based on what they think they like at that age. For example, students might pursue degrees in psychology or sociology because they want to help people. Others could pursue careers in visual arts like drawing or painting or performing arts such as dancing or singing because that is what they enjoy doing the most. What good does it do to earn degrees in careers in which there are no or limited job opportunities?

The truth about today's job market is that the careers that are most in demand or that pay very well require a strong foundation in science and, most of all, mathematics. For decades, if not longer, this has been America's weakness. When compared to most developed nations, American students lag behind their peers in both science and mathematics at all grade levels, especially at the high school level. This is why most American students are likely to enroll in academic programs that do not require students to take courses such as Calculus, Chemistry or Physics. Careers that are in demand, such as nursing, engineering or programming require students to pass high levels of math and science courses. The reality is that most American students are not ready or willing to put in the kind of effort that these courses demand.

Many high school students are not aware or properly informed about the enormous amount of new and interesting college careers, what those careers are about and the kind of job would they qualify to apply for. They are likely to choose careers based on what they have been exposed to or heard about through their peers and even television. For example, last month alone, at least three students have shared with me that they are planning to pursue a degree in criminal justice. When I asked then why, they did not know what to say. They did not know the requirements to be accepted into the program, the time it would take them to earn the degree or the places they would go to apply for a job after graduating. As strange as it may sound, what they knew about criminal justice is what they "learned" watching TV shows such as *CSI*, *Law and Order* and *Criminal Minds*.

The third college casualty happens when a college student gets into so much debt, that by the time he graduates and gets a job, a significant portion of his earnings will go into paying credit cards and student leans. College is not cheap! Being a full-time college student requires significant financial resources. Not only students must pay for their tuition but also other expenses such as books, room and board and transportation. Students who depend

> Students who depend on loans to pay for their college tuition and use credit cards for other college-related expenses could graduate college with debts as high as a car loan or even a mortgage.

on loans to pay for their college tuition and use credit cards for other college-related expenses could graduate college with debts as high as a car loan or even a mortgage. According to The Institute for College Access and Success (TICAS) Project on Student Debt, two-thirds (67%) of students graduating from American colleges and universities are graduating with some level of debt. The average borrowers will owe $26,600 by the time they graduate, just in student loans. One in ten (10%) will accumulate more than $40,000 in debt and one in a hundred (1%) will graduate with a crippling debt of $100,000 or more. In my opinion, a college degree with a high financial burden can definitely limit a young person's ability to live a quality life.

This financial issue hits home for me. My youngest child Deborah, in spite that she earned a full ride scholarship, managed to get herself into $30,000 in student loans and thousands in credit card debts. She left her home state of Florida to pursue a career in New York. The cost of living in Manhattan, New York is ridiculous and Deborah was a "spending machine." She was academically bright but financially "dull." There were years that she spent more than $500 eating out for breakfast, lunch and dinner. It was also very hard for her to restrain herself from buying things that she wanted. Deborah, like many other college students, admitted to having a need for immediate gratification. They want what they like and they want it now. She said to me, "Mom, if I could go back in time, I would manage my finances totally different." Although Deborah today has an excellent job in business management, three years after graduating college, she is still haunted by her debts. The amount of money she owes has become a barrier to total financial stability and freedom.

There are banks that offer students credit cards. Many students are not aware of the long-term negative financial impact of "plastic money." Their poor money management skills, combined with the need to have not what they need but what they want, leads them to max out their credit cards; and they usually do so in a short period of time. The high interest rates that most credit cards have grows their debt exponentially! They end up owing much more than they can afford to pay. They are in debt before graduating! By the time they complete their college education, these college credit cards debts affect their ability to support themselves.

There are several reasons why students get into debt. The most common one is that they do not know how to apply for "free money" or "gift-aid." By free money, I mean financial aid that does not require students to pay back such as merit-based or need-based scholarships. Getting gift-aid does not always come easy. Students must not only spend significant time searching for scholarships but also be able and willing to complete their application processes – and that is a lot of paper work! Many of these scholarships, especially the ones that are granted based on merit, require students to fill out forms, write essays, submit letters of recommendation and sometimes present evidence of quality academic work. On the other hand, student loans are not merit-based and their application process is definitely easier, especially when parents co-sign. They do not require students to do more than - fill out the loan application.

By now, I hope you have a better understanding of the purpose of this book. I am doing whatever it takes to prevent you from becoming one more college casualty. This is why we titled this book, *College Casualties: Twelve Competencies to Avoid Becoming One.* If you allow me to, I will like to provide you with twelve proven-to-work competencies that can prevent you from becoming one more college casualty.

FROM DEBORAH TO YOU

Hi! I am Deborah Ferrer. I would like to take this opportunity to reach out to any high school or college student reading this book. Although I succeeded at completing my college degree, I was almost a college casualty.

I enrolled as a Fine Arts student at first because I was following my passion for the visual arts. However, I realized that a degree in Fine Arts could not open doors to high in-demand jobs. How could I channel my skills as an artist and still get a job that could provide for my financial needs? I decided to reapply to seek out a different degree. I was essentially starting over! On top of that, I enrolled in a five-year program that would allow me to become a licensed architect. By then, I had already been in college for two years. How would I finance another five years? While this was a calculated risk, I was terrified!

Although I was the recipient of merit-based scholarships that paid for my tuition and books, I still needed a significant amount of money to pay for school supplies, housing and all the daily necessities of life. Well, housing was the biggest expense; I did live in New York City after all. Even after splitting my rent with a roommate, I still had to pay almost $9,000 a year in housing alone. Since I was an adult, I thought that renting a place was my first major investment in my education, and therefore my future. I was proud of it! To cover these expenses I maintained both, a full time and a part time job.

I admit that I was too liberal with my disposable income. I was living beyond my means at times, and I, like many of you, had to count on some kind of financial help from my mother. To support that kind of life, year after year, I got myself deeper and deeper into student loans and credit cards debts. However, the time came where I had to grow out of living in a state of perpetual financial crisis.

I learned one day that I had to be more resourceful with my money. I sat down to analyze my financial life and create a budget. I learned that, on average, I was spending more than $500 in meals. I also noticed that, in more than one occasion, I spent almost $900 eating at cafés and restaurants while I was on campus. This was a shock to me! It explained why I could not afford my electrical bill. It was time for a change. There are times in life that we must make bold moves. I had to delay that sense of immediate gratification and understand the cost of sustaining a life.

I discovered that I could spend a fraction of what it costs to eat in restaurants by buying groceries instead. I started preparing my meals at home. To save on rent, I even moved from Manhattan to Brooklyn, a 30-minute subway ride from my school. This financial awareness influenced everything from what kind of phone I would have, how often I would go to movies or how much I would spend on transportation.

In spite of all these financial changes, I still graduated with a $30,000 student loan debt and several thousands in credit cards responsibilities. Let me be honest with you. A part of me believes that these debts could have been significantly smaller if I had been more aware of the cost of living. I made many financial decisions that I am still paying for to this day.

After graduation, I was able to consolidate my student loan debts, reducing my monthly payment to an affordable amount. I have done the same with the foolish credit cards that I somehow qualified for in spite of being just a college student. Like thousands of college graduates, I have learned to live with and manage my college-related debts. I know two things - I am not defined by my income or my debts and no one, absolutely no one, can take away my college education.

As a college graduate in her twenties, I believe that, *College Casualties: Twelve Competencies to Avoid Becoming One,* is a book that could provide you with the insight, knowledge and strategies to avoid becoming a college casualty. I am sure that it can also help you develop the mental frame of reference, or way of thinking, that could improve your quality of life both in college and after graduation. If you have come this far, I invite you to discover the competencies outlined in this book so you can go even further. There will be times that you will stumble; but failure is not final or fatal! Learn from your mistakes, and more importantly, learn from mine.

Competency # 1

OVERCOMING CHALLENGES

Students recognize, understand and know how to overcome their personal life challenges.

"Life always throws unplanned situations in our way. I strongly believe that the best way to 'take on' these situations is to recognize what they are, understand why they happen and then accept that things might not come out as planned. We must tell ourselves to move forward even if things get harder than before. Everyone on this earth faces all kinds of challenges; of course, not all challenges are the same, some are bigger than others are. I have learned that as challenges come our way, we will grow and learn new things, not only about ourselves but also about the world that we live in." - Jimena Moreno

According to the United States Declaration of Independence, there are three unalienable rights given to all human beings by their Creator – the right to live, be free and pursue happiness. Out of these three rights, the one that gets my attention the most is the right to pursue happiness. More than anything in this world, I want to be happy! At the same time, in my almost 60 years of life, I have learned that facing challenges is part of life and people can experience happiness (or contentment) in spite of those challenges. In Steve Maraboli's words, "Happiness is not the absence of problems; it's the ability to deal with them."

> People like you and I have the opportunity to decide if we are to enrich ourselves with the fruits of a life challenge, or take that challenge as a poison and toxic presence in our lives.

He also believes that challenges in life can either enrich or poison a person. People like you and I have the opportunity to decide if we are to enrich ourselves with the fruits of a life challenge, or take that challenge as a poison and toxic presence in our lives. Most of us are either on our way to a new challenge, in the middle of it, or just coming out of one. It is for this reason that I believe that recognizing, understanding and knowing how to overcome personal challenges should be the first of the twelve competencies to avoid becoming one more college casualty, that is, one more student who drops out of college, earns a degree that is not in demand or graduates college with unbearable debts.

For the purpose of this book, the definition of a challenge is an unwelcomed and harmful matter or situation that we must deal with and overcome. Students like you are likely to face numerous and very distinct kinds of challenges and the first step is to identify what the challenge is. For example, there are students who struggle in school. They might lack the reading, math or maybe writing skills to do well in advanced classes. Some students might want to enroll in an Advanced Placement (AP) Calculus course but fear failing because their math skills are not at the level they need to be in order to do well in a class like that. Based on previous negative academic experiences, some students are convinced that they do not have what it takes to enroll in classes that can better prepare them for a successful college career. Students who are facing challenges regarding school should learn from them and grow by reaching out to the right resources. For example, keeping your parents and teachers informed about your struggles puts them in a position where they can better help you. Think of your elders as your personal facilitators of life; they can connect you to the right people if you need tutoring or extra help in a certain subject.

There are also students who are facing painful situations at home. Parents are not getting along and in your opinion, "they are just looking for any excuse to start a big argument." Sadly, you cannot do anything about it. The situation at home becomes unbearable to the point that they decide to divorce. Did you know that 50% of all the children born to married parents experience their parents' divorce before they reach 18 years old? If you are one of those students, you are not alone. You represent half of your generation experiencing the painful separation of parents. According to experts in the field of child development, students whose parents get divorced are more likely to suffer short and long-term emotional, physical and social damage than those whose parents stay together. These damages can have a negative impact on their ability to do well in school. This is when you have to be proactive about how you deal with a situation like that. There will be residual emotional damage that can follow you into college. I strongly encourage you to believe that you do not have to face a family problem alone. For those difficult moments, forming a positive and productive connection with one of your superiors or even a peer is essential to overcoming most personal challenges.

All sorts of social problems confront students, especially at the high school level. Students might live in home environment, or in neighborhoods, overloaded with negative social forces. They might have unwanted connections with people who engage in anti-social or aberrant behaviors. These behaviors include gang-affiliation, drug or alcohol abuse and child neglect or abuse. Students, who in spite of these unsurmountable challenges want to do well in school, not only will they have to fight temptations, but also suffer rejection, forcing them to become "loners" in their pursuit of a quality education.

To avoid giving up on their dreams about pursuing a post-secondary education or to prevent becoming a college casualty, students must clearly identify the challenge that threatens their ability to succeed academically. It is practically impossible for anyone of us to jump over barriers or fight forces that we cannot see or identify. You cannot be clueless regarding what is going on! Can you clearly state or describe the problem or problems that are affecting your academic life right now?

Identifying the challenge is not enough; students need to understand it. Understanding a challenge requires that people know the leading cause or reason behind the problem and most of all, the impact that the challenge is having in their lives. Can you explain why that problem came about? How is that problem affecting your academic life?

Lastly, students must learn and be able to implement strategies to overcome their challenges. What good does it do to identify and describe a problem if we do not look for a solution? People who only talk and whine about their problems are simply having a "pity party." You do not have time for that! What are you planning to do or not do to alleviate your situation? What strategies can help you achieve academic success in spite of the negative circumstances that surround you? Whom can you talk to about your problem?

The three vital steps that you could take to overcome your challenges are:

1. Embrace a victor and not a victim attitude –do not feel sorry for yourself!

2. Connect with the right people, individuals who can help you be a better person.

3. Develop a plan on how to deal and overcome your challenge with the assistance of people who understand your situation.

Young people who view themselves as victims of their circumstances are likely to feel sorry for themselves, feel helpless and do nothing to overcome their challenges. The "pobrecito yo" [Poor me] attitude is alive. People with this attitude usually use their challenges as an excuse to say, "I can't." On the other hand, students who embrace a victor attitude do not feel sorry for themselves; they have hope and do whatever it takes to experience victory over their negative circumstances. The "Claro que puedo" [Sure I can] attitude is alive! In addition, those who take on a victor's attitude are more likely to

> A person with a victor thinking is far more likely to inspire generosity in others than someone who plays the role of a victim.

attract the kind of help they really need. You want people to help you not because you are a victim and they feel sorry for you, but because in spite of your situation, you remain positive and proactive. A person with a victor thinking is far more likely to inspire generosity in others than someone who plays the role of a victim.

Connecting with the right people is extremely important. There is a saying in Spanish that says, "Dime con quién andas y te diré quién eres." This means, "Tell me who you hang out with and I will tell you who you are." Your relationships will likely determine your destiny. Someone once said, "Relationships, like elevators, can take you up or down." Identify, understand, and strategize around your relationships as well. Sometimes disconnecting from someone is just as important as connecting with the right person. You have a choice as to whom you hang out with and determine if they are contributing to, or detracting from, your ability to succeed in life. Well-qualified teachers and professors, school administrators and parents are looking out for your best interests. Motivated peers that excel in school are also great people for you to look up to. I have always enjoyed the proverb that says, "Be the change you want to see in the world." Seek out those people whom you can admire and whom you want to be like. Their influence alone can potentially be life altering.

Although seeking help from people who know how to help you is crucial, not everyone who cares about you has the knowledge and skills to assist you; therefore, you must be extra careful whom you approach. The bottom line here is that we all need help to overcome our life challenges, and we have to not only identify the challenge, but also identify a path towards a solution. When we are in the dark, any piece of good advice is all we need to improve our situation.

It is not always easy to develop a strategy to overcome certain challenges. When I was a college student in Puerto Rico, it was very difficult (or impossible) for me to complete my homework assignments or study for a test at home. My father was an alcoholic. He was at home most of the time because his condition did not allow him to retain a job. He was also verbally and physically abusive towards my mom, my siblings and myself. At the age of 15, for the first time, I clearly identified my father's alcoholism as a threat to my academic success. It took me 15 years to recognize the problem and to understand that my situation was not "normal." Since I was a churchgoer, I learned from my church leaders not only the reasons behind my father's abusive behaviors but also the negative impact that his alcohol addiction was having on my entire life. I learned that my dad had a horrible childhood. He ran away from home and was homeless until he joined the army. His life experiences made him emotionally ill. Although none of this is an excuse to abuse alcohol and his family, it allowed me to understand the why behind his behaviors. I was determined to learn and put in place strategies to overcome the challenge of having and living with a violent alcoholic father. It was difficult for me to remove myself from that environment because of my age and my father's reluctance regarding getting professional help. When I started college at the age of 17, my strategy was to go to school every single day. I left my house at 7:00AM and stayed in my college campus for at least eight hours, until I was done with all my school responsibilities. I attended my classes, completed my homework assignments and had my three meals in campus. Since I did not have the financial resources to stay in the dorms, the college library became my daytime home. I went home to go to church and to sleep. I could not change my father, but I was able to minimize the negative impact that he was having on my academic life.

I must say that in life only one can win - either you or your challenge. Eagles are not able to soar high into the sky without the resistance of strong winds. Like eagles, students must learn how to rise above that resistance, using the wind of a challenge to fly. Rising above life challenges will require students to recognize, understand and overcome whatever challenge they are facing. To do that they must assume the attitude of a victor, connect with the right people and most of all, seek the advice and help  they need to achieve their goals and experience academic and life success. You will continue to face challenges all throughout your academic life. Become an expert in overcoming them! This first competency will not only prevent you from becoming a college casualty but it will also help you to succeed in life.

Competency # 2

REACHING PROFICIENCY

Students increase their reading, writing and math levels of proficiency.

"Many times during a week at school I hear, 'When are we ever going to use this?' or 'Why are we even learning this?' The best and must simple answer is, 'You will definitely never need this in a minimum wage job. Is that what you want?' What teenagers my age do not understand is that reading, writing, mathematics ...are very important and arguably the most needed academic subjects for college success. The same way that it is very difficult to drive a car with a flat tire, it is very difficult to achieve academic success when you are 'low' in any of these academic areas." - Hesiquio Ballines

One of the leading reasons for the students' lack of academic success and low performance on high-stake standardized tests, from kindergarten to college, is their poor proficiency in three basic and yet very important academic areas - reading, math and writing. Too many American students are graduating high school without the knowledge and skills they need to enroll in a post-secondary educational program or enter the workforce. This is why increasing their proficiency in these three academic areas is one of the 12 competencies students must demonstrate to avoid becoming college casualties; that is, droppings out of college, earning degrees in fields with limited job opportunities or graduating college with chocking debts.

> ...a quality education is what opens doors to a quality life and the educational level of its young citizens is what determines a nation's ability to compete in a global economy.

The Information Era, the era that we are in, is global, extremely competitive, highly technological and constantly changing. Different from previous eras, a strong determination and a strong work ethic alone no longer leads to a quality life. In this era, a quality education is what opens doors to a quality life and the educational level of its young citizens is what determines a nation's ability to compete in a global economy.

One of our nation's greatest challenges is that we are in the midst of an academic crisis. Mediocrity reigns and academic rigor is almost non-existent in many of our schools. According to the 2011 TIMSS (Trends of International Math and Science Study) report, 4th and 8th grade students from Korea, Singapore, Hong Kong-CHN, Japan and the Russian Federation outperformed students from the United States of American, in both science and mathematics.

The 2013 NAEP (National Assessment of Educational Progress) report states that 48%, 54%, 78% and 83% of Asian, White, Hispanic and African American 8th grade students are reading below grade level. In mathematics, 40% of Asian, 55% of White, 79% of Hispanics and 84% of African American 8th students performed below grade level in mathematics.

This lack of reading and math proficiency is also prevalent at the states' accountability tests. For example, 28%, 32%, 62% and 71% of Asian, White, Hispanic and African American students failed the reading portion of the

2013 PSAE (Prairie State Assessment Exam), an assessment that 11th grade students in the state of Illinois take every year. During this same assessment, 24%, 35%, 64% and 79% of Asian, White, Hispanic and African American failed the math portion of the test.

As you can see, at the national and state levels, the lack of proficiency in reading and mathematics is more apparent among Hispanics and Blacks. It is depressing and unacceptable and a cause for great concern. Hispanics and Blacks are the two largest minorities in the United States. In the state of Illinois for example, Hispanics and Blacks combined are almost half of the student population.

According to the 2013 ACT report, less than 50% of Hispanic and African American students met any of the college-readiness benchmarks, which means that they are not ready or prepared to take college-level courses such as English Composition,

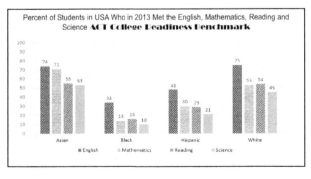

College Algebra, Biology or Social Sciences. Few students and parents are aware that this lack of college readiness also

means lack of career readiness. Although not every high school graduate plans to attend college, the majority of the fastest-growing jobs that only ask for a high school diploma, require the same knowledge and skills expected to start a college career. These kinds of jobs usually pay more than the minimum salary and provide opportunities for career advancement.

This is why a very large percentage of high school graduates, who enroll in our community colleges, must take remedial classes. I am not surprised because many years ago I was one of them. Although I graduated high school with a GPA of 4.0, my reading and math scores on the College Board Entrance Test disqualified me to take real college classes. I had to enroll in remedial courses for an entire year. Like me, many students have to learn through these remedial courses what they should had learned in high school, but at a faster pace. Students end up investing time, money and energy in courses that "don't count" towards the degree that they are pursuing. Faced with this reality, too many of them quit and dropout. Thank God, I stayed and prevailed.

The fact is that no matter how motivated students are to pursue a college career, their scores on college entrance tests such as the ACT, are used to decide the classes they will take, the degrees they will qualify to pursue and the amount of financial aid they will receive. For example, at the College of DuPage (COD), an ACT reading or math score less than 21 could place

a student in remedial courses. The motivation to pursue a college career, in my opinion, is like a car engine. Nevertheless, the lack of proficiency in any of these three key areas is like driving with a flat time. No matter how strong a car engine is, with a flat tire it cannot go anywhere.

Reaching reading proficiency is imperative. Students who are proficient readers can become life-long learners, which is an essential skill to stay employable in a constantly changing world. I am sure that you are aware that all academic subjects require students to read. The content of any academic subject, including mathematics, is presented in a written manner in order to ensure accuracy, consistency and equitable accessibility. More importantly, students cannot depend exclusively on what their teachers are explaining in class. Besides paying close attention to their teachers' lectures, students usually have to read and understand plenty of supplemental reading material. You cannot have your teachers 24/7 to help you learn everything you need to learn in a course, but you can always count on your books.

Reaching math proficiency is more important than ever in the history of our nation. Students who are proficient in mathematics are able to develop the critical-thinking and problem-solving skills needed to overcome academic and non-academic life challenges. In today's economy, most of the high-in-demand and high-paying jobs require a strong foundation in math. Math is at the core of all applied disciplines including computer, physics and chemistry sciences. Even students who pursue college careers that do not require a heavy dose of math courses have to take at least College Algebra and Statistics. I have met many students who cannot get their AA (Associate in Arts) degree because they have not been able to meet their minimum math requirements. They are stuck! A college student said to me the other day, "I am so closed to finishing my AA. What is holding me back is math. I love kids, so I want to become an elementary school teacher. I am worried that I will never be able to transfer and earn a teaching degree."

Students who reach writing proficiency can effectively communicate with others, which is a must-have capacity to work in environments that require collaboration. Effective communication is key to our ability to make our world a better place for all. There is a Spanish saying that states, "Las palabras se las lleva el viento," which means that, "Words can be blown away by the wind." Nevertheless, what you put in writing stays forever. High school classes such as English Language Arts, World History and college courses such as Psychology and Sociology require a significant amount of writing. Mastering the art of communicating in writing is pivotal in any academic career. Did you know that most grants and scholarships require students to write an essay as part of the application process? Therefore, a student's ability to write a high quality essay will likely determine the amount of financial aid, if any, he will get. Most of today's jobs, especially the ones that pay well, require employees to complete work-related forms, reports or write emails. Many employers are reporting frustrations with their employees' lack of writing skills. It is not a matter of handwriting. I have heard many of them say, "Even typed, I cannot understand what they write!"

To be successful in college, and later on in life, you must definitely do whatever it takes to be competent in these three academic areas. Your first step must be to find out your reading, writing and math levels of proficiency. Your best sources of information are your teachers' feedback, your GPA and most of all your standardized tests' scores. For example, let us start with reading. How well do you read? Are you reading below, at or above grade level? What was your reading score in the last standardized test you took?

Not long ago, I met Elizabeth, a very athletic 8th grade Latina girl in one of my parent workshops. Her parents asked her to come, hoping that she would get something out of the workshop. I immediately connected with her and like always, proceeded with a mini interview to offer some good academic advice. I asked her, "How well do you read? What is your reading and math levels of proficiency?" She did not know where she stood academically as well as she knew where she stood athletically. She had been taking the ISAT (Illinois Standard Assessment Test) every year since she was in third grade. She never cared about those tests' reports. I asked her parents to bring her sixth and seventh ISAT student reports next meeting. What a relief! We were happy to see that she was proficient in both reading and mathematics. I advised her to increase the amount of time she spends reading and engage in activities that can improve her math skills, just to be on the safe side.

As you can see through this example, once you know where you are, then you can decide where you want to be. This is the second step you must take to improve your reading, math and writing skills. You must set goals. As a veteran math teacher, I know that once you set your academic goals, the steps to improve in any academic area will require commitment, focus, hard work, feedback and strategizing.

When students commit to reaching academic goals, their daily actions demonstrate their determination to stay the course. Students who focus avoid all sorts of diversions when engaged in activities that will lead to reaching their proficiency targets. They work hard because they know that learning rigorous subjects demands great effort.

Students pay consideration to their teachers' feedback and use their performance on previous assignments and tests as a source of information to improve. Students who strategize use their teachers' feedback to answer the question, "What can I do differently to have better outcomes?" Then, they can stay the course.

Let us see how this applies. Let us meet José Rodriguez, a Salvadorian 16 year old senior student whose dream is to become a medical doctor, specifically a pediatrician. All careers in the medical field require a strong foundation in mathematics. Although math is not José's favorite subject, he decides to enroll in an AP Calculus class. He wants to earn a B or higher in class; and in order to earn some college credits, he needs to score a three or higher on the AP exam. As you can see, he knows what he wants and sets very specific goals to get it.

He will demonstrate his commitment by "pulling out all the stops" and doing whatever is necessary to reach his goals - at least a B in class and a three in the AP exam. He is determined! When he is attending class, doing his calculus homework, or studying for a test, he will resist the temptation to engage in activities that could divert his attention, such as texting, watching television or playing video games. He will work hard in order to learn the content of the course because he knows that learning Calculus will not be easy for him. He will seek feedback by paying attention to his homework and test results to see where he did well and where he needs to improve and learn from it. Finally, he will use the lessons learned through feedback to think and decide on new ways, or strategies, to improve his performance and reach his goals. I will write more about how to reach academic proficiency in Competency # 7.

In conclusion, reaching proficiency in reading, writing and mathematics is key to achieving academic success. There is no way around it! I believe that we can excel or at least get better in any academic area that we put our minds to. First, find out where you stand and then take the necessary steps to improve, that is, commit, focus, work hard, get feedback and strategize. Going to college is like driving cross-country on an interstate. Lack of proficiency in reading, writing or math is like driving with low air or worse, with a flat tire. If that is your case, do not stay there. Do something about it soon!

Strategies to Reach Academic Proficiency

1. Find out where you are. What are your current reading, math and writing levels of proficiency?

2. Decide where you want to be. What levels of proficiency do you want to reach?

3. Commit yourself to reach your proficiency goals.

4. Focus on your goals and avoid distractions.

5. Work as hard as you can to reach your proficiency goals.

6. Seek feedback to see how much you are improving.

7. Think and decide on new ways, or strategies, to improve your performance even more.

Dr. Lourdes Ferrer

Competency # 3

COMPLETING HOMEWORK

Students complete their daily homework assignments with integrity.

"After a long day at school, coming home to do homework can be a real drag. You sit in your seat for eight 50-minute classes, listening to the teacher go on and on about things that most of the time you do not even understand. To top it off, they give you so much homework that you barely get any time to rest at home. Let us face it though, without all the work they give us, there would not be a challenge at all. What is the fun in life without overcoming all these challenges? To stay on the right path towards success, I believe it is extremely necessary that students complete their homework assignments daily and to do them with integrity. This is true not only with school but with everything in life." - Alexis Davila

Let us face it – doing homework every day is one of the most challenging aspects in a student's life. I believe that doing homework is to academic success what sports practice is to a championship. The same way that

athletics cannot win a soccer championship without intense and daily practice, students cannot achieve academic success without honest and daily homework completion. This is why making homework completion part of your daily routine and doing so with integrity is one of the twelve competencies to avoid becoming a college casualty, which means, dropping out of college, earning degrees that are not in demand or graduating with overwhelming debts.

Students who complete their daily homework assignments without cutting corners do better in school and perform better on tests than those who do not. They are likely to have a good Grade Point Average (GPA) and score high on standardized tests such as the ACT and SAT. Like any sport, it will require willingness to put in the necessary effort. The question is, "How can students overcome their unwillingness, especially after a whole day in school?"

First, students must clearly see the value of homework and how doing it helps them reach their academic goals. Doing homework has many benefits. It allows students to pick up information that they could have missed in class and fill in content gaps. Homework assignments also allow students to reinforce what they learned in class so they can be better prepared to do well on any test. For example, your peers or your teachers can help you when you are stuck solving a math problem in class. After class, things are different; like in a testing situation, you are on your own. Your ability to get the right answers will tell you if you are ready to ace that test! If you see that you are not ready, then you have enough time to get the help you need.

Second, homework assignments can provide teachers with information or feedback regarding how well students learned the lesson. I know this as a fact because I was a high school math teacher for many years. My students' reactions towards homework or their ability to solve the math problems was my way of knowing if my lesson plans were right and if my teaching strategies were on target. There were numerous times that I had to re-teach or modify a lesson plan and even postpone the date of the test because, based on my students' reactions or homework performance, I knew they were not ready. In my opinion, homework assignments are the best way for teachers to assess the quality and learning outcomes of their instruction.

Third, students who complete their homework assignments on their own, on time and on a consistent basis develop and strengthen many of the character traits that are essential to excel in school. In my opinion, the most important character trait is discipline. Discipline gives you the fuel to do what you need to do, even if you do not want to do it; it is the ability to deny yourself. Students who learn discipline are able to put their responsibilities ahead of their desires.

> Discipline gives you the fuel to do what you need to do, even if you do not want to do it; it is the ability to deny yourself. Students who learn discipline are able to put their responsibilities ahead of their desires.

Discipline helps you choose to complete your homework instead of watching your favorite TV show or studying for a test instead of taking a nap. It is very difficult or maybe impossible to accomplish anything of significance in life without discipline.

There are seven strategies than can help you make homework a less stressful and maybe more gratifying experience. First, try to create a home environment that allows you to focus on your homework assignments. For example, turn off the TV and put your smart phone on silent. You must avoid distractions because focus is the key to a productive homework time. If you cannot create that environment at home, you will have to do what I did when I was a college student. Find a place away from home where you can do your homework assignments free of distractions. In my case, that place was the library. I enjoyed the silence and the company of students who were doing exactly what I was doing – pursuing academic success.

Second, establish a regular homework schedule. A regular schedule will help you make homework completion a daily habit. I recommend that you set the time for the late afternoon or early evening rather than just before bed. Just before bedtime can affect your ability to fall asleep, especially if your homework assignments required a lot of reasoning. Doing homework beyond your sleeping time will definitely affect your academic performance. Medical doctors, especially pediatricians, are reporting that the lack of sleep is having a negative impact in American students' ability to learn.

Third, try to do your homework on your own. Seek help only if you need to. Completing homework with the assistance of others will create dependency and prevent you from developing the self-confidence you need to engage in higher academic content. You must also remember that you will be on your own when the test comes. Your homework performance is your best way of knowing, ahead of time, if you are ready to do well on the test. To reach your academic goals, eventually you will have to learn to believe in your potential to learn.

Fourth, avoid being negative. Make homework time a positive experience – At least try! I believe homework time should be a whining-free zone. Expressions such as - "I can't", "I won't" or "I don't" should not be in your vocabulary! A negative attitude towards homework, your teachers or school creates a lot of stress and stress will definitely have a negative impact on your willingness and ability to learn.

Fifth, organize your homework assignments in a more productive way. For many students, homework can be an overwhelming experience. You might be taking Geometry, American History, Biology and Spanish and getting homework from all these classes at the same time. Which assignment do you do first? Which one is easier? All of these questions might be screaming inside of your head. Homework time should also be a stress-free zone. Break

> Many students are not aware that teachers in general enjoy students who ask questions regarding their homework assignments because it shows interest in what they are teaching.

your homework load into smaller pieces and deal with it a piece at a time. I would do the easier ones first to feel that I am moving forward and tackle the ones that are due earlier to avoid "late fees." You know what I mean. In Puerto Rico we say, "Do not leave for tomorrow what you can do today." Doing your homework assignments sooner rather than later will take away a lot of stress.

Sixth, seek help from your teachers. Do not be afraid to approach your teachers for extra help if you find yourself struggling with your homework. Many students are not aware that teachers in general enjoy students who ask questions regarding their homework assignments because it shows interest in what they are teaching. Most teachers are willing to go an extra mile to help a student who is seeking help. I must confess that when I was a high school math teacher, I tended to pay a little extra attention to students that came to me before class or that stopped me in the halls to say, "Ms. Ferrer, I had a real hard time with my math homework last night." When students ask questions about homework during class, classmates also benefit. The challenges you are facing might be the same ones your classmates are facing. You win, your classmates win and even the teachers win. As I said before, a question regarding homework is the best way for teachers to know the outcomes of their instruction.

Finally yet importantly, use technology to make homework completion an easier daily task. The internet can easily provide you with any kind of information you need to complete any assignment. For example, if you need information of the true meaning of the "Cinco de Mayo," just "google it." You will read documents, see pictures and even watch videos about it. My daughter Deborah informed me that certain higher education institutions like the prestigious M.I.T. (Massachusetts Institute of

Technology) actually publish their lectures via YouTube. Could you believe that? Through the internet, she was able to access online libraries from around the world and download files for her research projects.

If you then need to write a paper about your research, use the tools in Microsoft Word to your advantage. Word will count the words, identify grammatical mistakes and even let you know when you are using passive sentences. There are also numerous websites designed to help you with your homework assignments, especially math. The Khan Academy, for example, has thousands of videos that explain how to solve any kind of math problem. In Competency # 12, I will further explain how technology can help students attain their academic goals.

In conclusion, making homework completion a daily routine, and doing it with integrity, is key to academic success. Period! On the other hand, for most students doing homework is a very challenging academic exercise. Once students internalize the benefits of completing their home assignments, they must implement strategies to make it less nerve wrecking. Besides making a homework schedule (and sticking to it), organizing their assignments and creating the right environment, they must try to do their assignments on their own. Using technology can really help students make homework completion an easier task. Maintaining a positive attitude towards homework and seeking help from their teachers when confronted with problems is also essential. Not doing so is a disservice not only to you but also to your peers and even your teachers. Since homework completion will always be an essential component of a student's life, making it a positive experience will prevent students from becoming one more college casualty.

Homework Strategies

1. Create a home environment that allows you to focus.
2. Establish a regular homework schedule.
3. Do your homework on your own.
4. Avoid being negative.
5. Organize your homework assignments in a productive way.
6. Seek help from your teachers when needed.
7. Use technology to make homework completion an easier task.

Competency # 4

ESTABLISHING CONNECTIONS

Students establish productive connections with people who can provide assistance when needed.

"As a student, I am always trying to show or prove to my teachers how important education is to me. I feel that making good connections with them will help me be a better student. When I feel connected with my teachers, my classes are easier. I enjoy class and feel comfortable asking questions. Every time I have a difficult time understanding something, I look for help until I find it. My first choice is the teachers. I instantly look for them because they are the best qualified to give me all the information that I need."   -

Karina Callegos

In my 30-plus years of experience working with high school students, I have noticed that the students who need help the most are the ones who seek help the least, and vice versa. I always ask myself, "why?" Is it fear? Is it pride? I know that it is very difficult, if not impossible, to achieve academic success without the council and assistance of teachers, guidance counselors, school administrators, high-achieving peers and, in some cases, family members. It is arrogant and

maybe stupid to think that we can accomplish big things in life totally on our own. That is why pursuing positive and productive connections with the right people is one of the twelve competencies for students to avoid becoming a college casualty; that is, dropping out of college, earning degrees that are not in demand or graduating college with overwhelming debts.

Trying to go through your high school and college career completely on your own is like driving from New York to California without a GPS. You are likely to get lost! Having a person on your side, who is there for you when you need it, is like carrying your personal GPS. How cool is that! That person knows where you are and how to get you where you need to be in your academic career path.

There are several reasons why many students are pretty much on their own throughout their academic lives. First, they might not know that it is perfectly normal and even necessary to seek help. Like athletes, students need some sort of coaching from people who are there to provide advice or guidance when needed. I have heard many high school students say silly statements such as, "I can do this on my own." "I do not need anyone's help." Maybe they think that seeking help is a sign of weakness or inability.

There are students who fear that their peers will perceive them as teachers' pets. They care more about what their peers think or say about them than the benefits of having connections with the right people. Not long ago a very studious high school student said to me, "Others students make fun of me every time I greet my teachers at the halls or ask how they are doing. My classmates criticize me when I approach a teacher to ask a question or get some advice. I want my teachers to know me and see that I really care about my education; so, I learned not to care what my peers think or say about me."

I have also observed that some students believe that no one in their schools cares about their education. In their minds, the teachers are there just to teach and test; the guidance counselors are there to decide students' schedules; and the administration is there to do their administrative duties. They are convinced that no one besides their friends will care about their personal and academic wellbeing. They only connect or establish relationships

> Students who hold this belief are wrong! Most teachers, guidance counselors, school social workers, etc., choose these types of careers because they like kids and enjoy making a difference in the lives of young people.

with their same-age peers. As one student once said to me, "Everyone that works in this school is here just for the money. They don't care about me and they don't care about any of us." Students who hold this belief are wrong! Most teachers, guidance counselors, school social workers, etc., choose these types of careers because they like kids and enjoy making a difference in the lives of young people.

Learning how to establish positive and productive connections with teachers or other professionals who can provide some kind of assistance when needed is imperative.

By positive, I mean that the relationship contains mutual trust, respect and collaboration. By productive, I mean that you get something out of the relationship, you get a product. For example, a student not only gets along with his Biology teacher but he also gets some kind of assistance when he faces challenges in class. Teachers can go beyond the scope of their teaching duties to help you write an essay paper, understand the main idea of an article or create a Power Point presentation. They can provide you with a letter of recommendation or some guidance when deciding which courses to take or which career to pursue in college. Teachers can also give you some advice regarding how to handle a personal or family problem that is affecting your academic life.

People who do great things in life usually recognize those who helped them achieve their goals. Successful individuals have a long list of people to thank for their success.

Students have a greater chance to overcome their challenges and reach their goals when they have connections with people who have the knowledge and desire to help them when needed.

Here are seven strategies that can help you establish connections with the right people. First, accept the idea that you cannot achieve your academic and career goals on your own. You need help! People who do great things in life usually recognize those who helped them achieve their goals. Successful individuals have a long list of people to thank for their success.

Second, recognize who are the right people to establish positive and productive relationships. Seek connections or rub shoulders with individuals who have a caring spirit and have abundance of what you need. You might need inspiration, motivation, advice, knowledge or skills. If they care and have what you need, do whatever it takes to connect with them. Let me give you an example. Eric, a senior student, is struggling in his Physics class. He is determined to pass Physics with at least a B to qualify for an engineering college program. His teacher's wealth of knowledge is exactly what Eric desperately needs to pass the class. If Eric has a good connection with his Physics teacher, his teacher is likely to stay after school, come early and even spend his lunchtime helping Eric understand the concepts or problems that he does not understand. Trust me! Teachers are likely to go beyond their duties to help students with whom they have a good student-teacher relationship.

Third, maintain a positive attitude towards school, teachers and schoolwork. Teachers, counselors, school administrators and academic coaches like myself, do not enjoy helping students who criticize their teachers, dislike their schools or complain about their school-related responsibilities. I personally do not spend my time, energy or knowledge with whiners. I am willing to care and share my expertise with students who are determined to overcome their challenges and excel in school. This highlights the difference between victim mentalities versus victor mentalities. A victor can see the horizon ahead, and can transcend above the "I can't" attitude.

> I personally do not spend my time, energy or knowledge with whiners. I am willing to care and share my expertise with students who are determined to overcome their challenges and excel in school.

Fourth, establish connections as early as possible in the school year. Sometimes students wait too long. They try to connect with the people who can help them only when they need immediate assistance or are totally lost. For example, Serena, a high school junior, might try to approach her English Language Arts teacher when she knows she is failing the class, few weeks before the end of the course. Too late! There are senior students who meet with their guidance counselors to get information about scholarships a month before graduation. By that time, the dead line for most scholarships are due, leaving you with fewer options and opportunities. Counselors and teachers will not be able to help you on such short notice.

Fifth, recognize that the people you will need to seek out will come in all shapes, sizes, age groups, and cultures. Judging a book by its cover can only lead to missed opportunities. It can prevent you from meeting the person who can offer valuable advice or a fresh perspective. Your best ally might not fit into your definition of what is "cool." He (or she) might be an unpopular and strict teacher, a guidance counselor who speaks with a heavy accent or a school administrator four times your age. It does not matter! If they can bring value to your life, by all means, pursue a productive relationship with them.

Sixth, when you want to connect with someone, start with introducing yourself gracefully. Smile a lot! Give a firm handshake. Look at the person's eyes. Speak clearly and do not mumble. Say something positive about yourself and clearly state what you admire or need from that person.

Make yourself likeable! A few hours ago, I had a phone conversation with a young Latina high school girl. With a sweet and happy voice, she said her name and immediately shared with me her desire to achieve greater academic success. "I know that you help students improve their writing skills. I also heard that you help them improve their ACT math scores," she said to me. Then she added, "Can you please help me too? Can you be my academic coach?" Who can say no to that? She caught my attention and grabbed my heart. I immediately said yes. Sometimes your personality can be your best asset. How you come across to your potential mentors (advisors or counselors) is key to getting their attention. Make them like you!

Seventh, make sure that your connections (academic coach, teachers, guidance counselors, etc.) get appropriate information about any situation that could affect or is affecting your academic or personal life. The people who are counselling or guiding you need to know about any challenge that threatens your academic progress. For example, let the teachers who are connected with you know if something is going on in your family like the death of a close relative, parents' divorce, a parent job loss, etc., which may have a negative impact in your schoolwork and/or behavior. These teachers will surely help you cope with these adverse circumstances and help you stay on track.

Positive and productive connections are the backbone of your academic career. Being a student is not easy. Pursuing a high-in-demand career is a very challenging endeavor – a very complicated route. Most students never start; and the few who do, never finish because they get lost in the way. Although you are in the driver's seat when it comes to your education, a good GPS, or the right connections will definitely help you get where you need to be.

Strategies to Establish Positive Connections

1. Accept the idea that you cannot achieve your academic goals on your own.

2. Recognize who are the right people to connect with.

3. Maintain a positive attitude towards school, teachers and schoolwork.

4. Establish connections as early as possible in the school year.

5. Recognize that good connections might not fit into your definition of what is "cool."

6. Introduce yourself gracefully and make yourself likeable!

7. Keep your connections informed about situations that

Dr. Lourdes Ferrer

Competency # 5

BUILDING CHARACTER

Students demonstrate the character traits that are conducive to academic and life success.

"Many students have the ability to do great things but fail because they lack the drive to do so. I see this lack of motivation among all my peers, no matter their grade level, every day at West Aurora High School. Many students would like to achieve great things in their school career such as joining a sport team, starting an afterschool club, or running to be part of the Student Council, but if they do not have respect for themselves or others, they will never be able to reach any of these goals. If students would just put forth the effort and stop relying so much on others to do things for them, then they would be able to achieve academic success and a superb quality of life. The pathway or road to this requires that students demonstrate the four character traits that are essential to academic and life success."
- Rodolfo Lozano Jr.

Have you ever seen a very athletic student who never made the final cut to join the school team? For example, a student who does not care about his grades, is disrespectful towards teachers or hangs out with the wrong crowd will have a hard time joining the soccer team, even if he is the best soccer player

> Dr. Albert Einstein said, "Most people say that it is the intellect which makes a great scientist. They are wrong. It is character."

in school. He has the gift to play but not the character traits to represent the school. Dr. Albert Einstein said, "Most people say that it is the intellect which makes a great scientist. They are wrong. It is character." That is why I believe that understanding and demonstrating the character traits that are conducive to academy success should be one of the twelve competencies to avoid becoming one more college casualty. A college casualty, in my opinion, is a student who drops out of college,

earns a degree that is not in-demand or graduates with an unsurmountable amount of debts.

A person's character is behind his or her actions. Actions are what we do, but our character traits (who we are) determine why we do them. Students who stand out academically do so because they have the drive or the desire to do what is right to achieve academic success. In my opinion, they are on "cruise control." Why? Parents or teachers do not need to "press the gas." Students with character are motivated to do what they need to do on their own accord. Out of the many positive character traits linked to academic success, I teach four traits that I consider significant to achieving success in school. These traits are responsibility, a smart-hard work ethic, persistence and the ability to delay personal gratification.

> Students who are responsible... hold themselves accountable for their own actions and do not make excuses, or blame others, for what they did or did not do.

Students, who are responsible or behave in a responsible manner, do not tend to let people down. If they agree to do something, they simply do it! They hold themselves accountable for their own actions and do not make excuses, or blame others, for what they did or did not do. Responsible students take care of their personal matters and do not rely on their parents or other people for things they are supposed to do themselves. This character trait allows students to follow guidelines and meet due dates. They do not cut corners!

Teachers love to teach responsible students. For example, if Carlos agreed to meet his peers at the school library after school, he will be there even if he gets an invitation to do something more fun. If Ruth did not study and failed a test, she will not say, "The teacher never covered that material in class." If Steve has to do some research about a certain topic, he will not ask or allow any of his peers to do the work for him. If Gabriella has to turn in a paper on a certain day, she will not "get sick" just to avoid seeing the teacher that day.

The second of the four character traits is a smart-hard work ethic. Students need to value both a smart and a hard work ethic. There is a difference between working smart and working hard. I have seen too many students, parents and even professionals putting great effort into goals without any results. They might be aiming at the right thing but in a wrong way. They are working hard, not smart. On the other hand, students who work hard in a smart way understand, believe and commit with a clear vision and specific target in mind.

It is very difficult to put smart effort in any academic subject without a clear understanding of the steps that precede or follow to reach mastery. For example, if Philip wants to enroll in an elite engineering program, he must know which math courses he must pass to qualify for the program. Students with a smart-hard work ethic believe in their ability to reach their goals. For example, Joe is likely to enroll in an AP Calculus class if he believes he has the knowledge and skills to pass the class. His belief

> Students who work hard in a smart way understand, believe and commit with a clear vision and specific target in mind.

will boost the confidence he needs to do well in a class like that. Working hard in a smart way will also require students to commit; that is, to do whatever it takes to reach their academic goals. For example, if George is committed to passing his Physics class with an A, he is willing to spend time doing his homework, participate in class and study for the tests, instead of spending his time engaged in distractions. He is committed. He is serious!

Persistence is the third character trait that you need to develop to excel in school and succeed in life. Students who are persistent usually also have a strong work ethic. When confronted with challenges, persistence empowers students to keep on going and not give up. You have heard the expression, "When the going gets tough, the tough gets going." In Deborah's words, "Failure is not final and success is not often a straight line. There are bumps on the road along the way, but it is up to us not to forget our vision, the objective of our goals and dreams. Therefore, persistence is the ability to surpass those bumps and failures by getting up again and moving forward."

I always advise students to be persistent only on things that will help them achieve their goals. Persistence is like money. Do not waste it on things that are not important. For example, I have seen too many students persisting on becoming friends with people

> Students who are persistent usually also have a strong work ethic. When confronted with challenges, persistence empowers students to keep on going and not give up.

who are not interested in school. They should instead invest their time and energy building relationships with peers who share their academic goals or adults who can assist them when needed.

You must understand that persistence does not mean doing the same thing repeatedly until you get it right. It is the very definition of insanity to think that doing the same thing will get you different results. If something did not work, persist but use a different strategy. I have seen many students that, instead of taking a prep-course, getting a tutor or joining a study group, they take the ACT repeatedly hoping to get a better score. Crazy! Part of persistence is being able to identify where your original strategy fell short, and where you succeeded. In Deborah's words, "Understanding the journey is just as important as understanding the destination."

The last but not least of the four character traits that you must develop is the ability to delay personal gratification. Some people are almost slaves to whatever thing, activity, person, etc. that brings immediate gratification. Sad, isn't it? Nevertheless, the reality is that most of the things that are valuable in life require sacrifice. Delayed gratification is an invaluable character trait because it gives students the ability to give up immediate pleasure for long-term benefits. For example, Richard will delay the fun of playing video games, posting pictures in histogram or texting friends, until he has completed all his homework assignments. I know that it is a sacrifice to deny yourself from immediate gratification. However, great goals always demand great sacrifices. Let us not forget that great sacrifices can give birth to great rewards.

A young woman brought her baby son to Robert E. Lee, the well-known Confederate general. She asked him, "What should I do to help my son succeed?" Robert E. Lee replied, "Teach him to deny himself." We can see this character trait in all our great athletes. None of them has reached greatness without painful practices and sore muscles. The pain they feel because of their hard work, to them, is like a badge of honor.

> Delayed gratification is an invaluable character trait because it gives students the ability to give up immediate pleasure for long-term benefits.

So many talented students accomplish so little in life. A very wise person once said, "Giftedness without character only leads to disaster." Therefore, no matter how smart you are, you must evaluate yourself to see if you have the character traits that lead to a meaningful and satisfying life. If you find yourself lacking any of the fours character traits mentioned in this Competency, seek help! When it comes to your education, you must sit in the driver's seat. However, the road that leads to high-in-demand careers are usually long. Your character will empower you to reach your academic destination because it will put you in cruise control. One of Beowulf quotes says, "Behavior that's admired is the path to power among people everywhere." Meet the expectations laid out for your success and you will find yourself empowered and motivated to conquer the next steps of your life.

Dr. Lourdes Ferrer

Competency # 6

BELIEVING IN THEMSELVES

Students believe in their potential to learn and expect themselves to achieve.

"I did not believe I had the ability to understand any of the content taught in class. Before and during the test, I knew I was going to fail. I did not know how I was going to show my mom a bad grade; however, I knew I had to! One day, my mom talked to me about what was going on with me in school and I explained to her that I did not understand anything that the teacher taught. I was struggling a lot! Later, she told me, 'You will be able to be a better student if you become your best advocate.' I have realized how much being my best advocate and believing in my potential has made me a better student, knowing that I am capable of accomplishing anything that I put my mind into doing." - Christian Ramirez

Would you start something you do not believe you can complete? Would you put effort into a project you do not expect to be a success? Definitely not! In my many years of experience as a high school math teacher, I saw a significant number of students who were convinced that they did not have the ability to pass my math class. From the beginning, they expected to fail. Their negative attitude towards math killed any desired to participate in class, do homework, or study for my tests only to reinforce their own false belief system. They set themselves up for failure. The bottom line is that students are less likely to read, complete their homework assignments, study for their tests, seek help from their teachers or do whatever it takes to do well in school, if they do not think their efforts will make a difference. If they believe they do not have the potential to learn, why should they bother? This is why believing in your ability to learn and expecting yourself to achieve your academic goals must be one of the twelve competencies to avoid becoming a college casualty.

I always tell students that belief is to academic success what fuel is to a car engine. No matter how powerful a car engine is, without fuel it cannot go anywhere. Your belief will fuel your potential to learn. Your level of belief will greatly influence your level of academic success. Take a moment to look at how far you have come. By now, you have faced several challenges and celebrated many successes. If  you had support in your endeavors, that is, involved parents and teachers who cared about your success, count those among your blessings. This is evidence of your success so far! You might not have any other choice but to believe in your ability to attain your goals.

Believing in your potential to learn can protect you from unavoidable negative forces that could cause you to give up on your academic goals. You must be aware of these forces so you can minimize, or eliminate, the negative impact that they can have on your academic career. The first of these negative forces, believe it or not, can come from home. There are parents who do not believe in their children's ability to learn and therefore, do not expect them to do well in any academic subject. They did not experience academic success when they were children and think that their children inherit their academic letdowns. During a parent-teacher conference, the father of a student who was struggling in my class said to me, "My son is not good in math because he does not have the brains to do so. He is like me. I hated math when I was in school. I will be happy if he just passes the

There are parents who do not believe in their children's ability to learn and therefore, do not expect them to do well in any academic subject. They did not experience academic success when they were children and think that their children inherit their academic letdowns.

class, so he does not have to repeat it again next year. However, I really appreciate your interest in helping my son." Unfortunately, this parent was not setting his son up for success. Parents are in the position to empower their children; however, not all parents are aware of their impact. My student lived up to those expectations! As you can see, that negative force can be a bar not raised high enough.

The second negative force can be the old, but still popular, Innate Ability theory. People who embrace this theory judge that innate ability alone determines what and how much students can learn. In other words, their genes will exclusively decide the level of academic success that they will experience in school. People who support this theory believe that some people can learn and some cannot.

I ask myself, "If students believe that they are one of those who cannot learn, why would they bother to get involved in activities that could improve their performance in school?"

According to Dr. Howard, the founder of the Efficacy Institute, "People who support the Innate Ability Theory believe that a person's ability is fixed at birth; that is, it cannot be changed. Failure or difficulty indicates limits in the individual's ability." I want to know that your ability to perform is not static like the length of your bones. It is more

"People who support the Innate Ability Theory believe that a person's ability is fixed at birth; that is, it cannot be changed. Failure or difficulty indicates limits in the individual's ability."

like a muscle because when exercised, it can grow and get stronger. Failure is not final either. Difficulty indicates that you have an opportunity to grow and learn. Academic challenges develop character without diminishing your value or sense of self-worth.

The third negative force that can have a negative impact in your ability to learn is people's adverse presuppositions about you as a student. Although it is wrong, in real life people are likely to judge others based on the way they look. People's negative assumptions about race or ethnicity adversely can affect both African-American and Hispanic students' ability to believe in themselves. The statistics show that these two ethnic groups are over-represented in low socio-economic neighborhoods, dead-end low-paying jobs, the penal system, and in lower academic tracks. These realities affect people's perceptions regarding these two minorities, which affects students' ability to believe that they can achieve more than what others of their same-race/ethnicity have achieved.

> People's negative assumptions about race or ethnicity adversely can affect both African-American and Hispanic students' ability to believe in themselves.

During a focus group conversation that I had with a group of Hispanic high school students, one student said, "When you are joking around with students, you hear sometimes jokes that say 'Come down and mow my lawn.' There are racist jokes like that. Mexicans mowing lawns, being janitors and stuff like that. It makes you think, what are you doing here? Why are you trying to complete school if that is what you might end up doing? That is where racism plays a role. It deteriorates your motivation and it does not help you want to try as hard as you should." Negative presuppositions are belief killers! That is why I strongly believe that students need tools to overcome these outside negative forces.

Students not only must believe in their ability to learn, but they must also set high academic expectation for themselves. Believing and expecting are two different things. Expecting is a step beyond believing. It demands action! For example, you might believe that you have the

ability to fix your room but do not take the steps to clean it because you do not expect yourself to do so.

Using the analogy of a car, I see setting high academic expectations like moving the transmission gearshift from parking to drive. A strong engine with a tank full of fuel will not move unless you change the transmission gearshift. Right? A bright high school student once said to me, "I know I can do better. If I really wanted to, I can get all A's and B's. However, I am satisfied with C's. As long as I pass my classes and get the minimum GPA to graduate high school, I am happy." As you can see, this student believed in his ability but did not expect himself to achieve. Believing in your ability to learn alone (or having fuel) does not lead to career success. Setting high academic expectations for yourself (or moving the transmission gearshift to drive) requires two very important things – great desire and a strong will to do whatever it takes to see realized what you already believe you can achieve.

The desire that leads to high expectations is a feeling that means longing for something. It is a very important emotion because humans, and in this case students, are likely to put a lot of effort only into goals that they have a great desire to accomplish. Students, for example, will need a lot of desire to excel in order to earn an A (or B) in an AP course or any class such as Physics or Chemistry. On the other hand, the will power that leads to high expectations is more than an emotion; is the faculty that allows students to decide on and initiate actions that lead to what they desire.

A strong will empowers students to take the action steps that lead to their academic success. Aiming for an A in rigorous academic courses, for example, will not only require great desire but also the will to take the necessary steps to attain that goal, such as religiously attending class, completing homework with integrity and spending numerous hours studying for the tests.

Let me give you another example. Few months ago, I learned about a student who publicly stated that he was aiming at a 30-plus ACT Composite Score. That is high! He believed he had the ability to score that high and expected himself to do so. He purchased study materials, took prep-courses and studied not for weeks, but for months. Most of his peers were astonished when they learned he scored a 32. I was not. As you can see, his actions demonstrated the desire and the will he had to score that high. He believed in his ability and expected himself to reach his ACT 30-plus goal.

In order to believe in your potential to learn and set high academic expectations for yourself, I recommend that you do the following. First, do not judge or see yourself through the lens of you parents or other relatives. Your parents are your parents and you are you. It is true that we inherit many physical traits from our parents. You might have your father's height and your mother's color of eyes. However, you do not have to inherit beliefs, attitudes and perceptions that can damage your ability to believe you can achieve a bright future. For example, you can be an awesome Mathematics Teacher even if your mother failed and hated math.

Second, reject the Innate Ability theory. You must publicly and boldly state that people can learn whatever they need to learn with effective effort. It is true that we are all different. For some students, doing math problems or writing an essay comes easy. Nevertheless, humans have the ability to learn or get better in anything that they are determined to do so. You might not be the best swimmer in the world or win an Olympic medal; but you can certainly learn how to swim. You might not be a mathematician; but you can certainly meet all the math requirements to achieve your career goals.

Third, do not internalize other people's negative expectations about your race or ethnicity. On the contrary, make the determination to become a stereotype-breaker, the proof that you are not what others might think you are. A high school girl wrote to me once, "I decided to take

Calculus even though I am the only Black student in that class. Most Black students are afraid to take it because they are afraid to fail. But I am determined to prove that Blacks can also excel in math."

In conclusion, it is commanding that you believe in your potential to learn and expect yourself to achieve. These two working together will drive the desire and the will you need to accomplish great things in life. You are the only vehicle that can take you where you need to be. Therefore, you must sit in the driver's sit when it comes to your own post-secondary education. Now you know that with enough fuel and the gearshift in the drive position, you are on your way to career success.

Dr. Lourdes Ferrer

Competency # 7

NURTURING THEIR INTELLIGENCES

Students understand and know how to increase their intelligences.

"As a junior at West Aurora High School, I have seen many students not participate in activities because they think they do not have the natural talent to succeed. I am talented in mathematics because I have nurtured it enough to participate in math competitions. For a fact, I know that I do not have any talent in singing. Just hear me sing and you will have your ear drums ruptured! I know that some people are more talented in certain areas than others; but we all have the ability to learn if we nurture it, feed it and make it grow. Students who do not believe in their potential to learn give up when they face challenges. They stop doing homework, studying for tests, and paying attention to the teacher during class. I strongly believe that students who do not nurture their ability to learn will never reach their full potential and goals in life." - David Ballines

There are people who strongly believe that not all individuals are born with the ability to learn. They think that a person's genetic composition solely determines what and how much he or she will learn. In other words, their intelligence and level of academic success is pre-established since conception. I totally disagree with people who hold that belief. I  support the idea that today's neuroscientists hold - that the amount of effort that people put into learning something new is more powerful than the genes they inherit from their parents. For example, nature gave the apple seed the potential to become an apple tree. However, without nurturing that seed, that is, providing soil, water and light, it will never become what nature intended that seed to be. If we apply this truth to us, nature gave us all the ability to learn and become intelligent human beings. However, if we do not nurture our genetic capacity to learn we will not experience the level of intelligence nature gave us the potential to reach.

Experts in the field of education consistently state that becoming more intelligent, attaining proficiency in any academic subject or reaching your academic goals is a matter of nature and nurture working together. That is why understanding and knowing how to increase our intelligences, or ability to learn, is one of the twelve competencies that could prevent students from becoming college casualties.

According to brain development scientists, the degree of connectivity between brain neurons determines how intelligent a person is. In other words, the number and strength of connections between your brain cells (neurons) will decide what and how you can and will learn. This is great news because you as a student have the power to become smarter; that is, to become more intelligent! The more you challenge your brain, the more neurological connections your brain will make. It is my belief that students can nurture their intelligence if they set clear goals, believe in their ability to learn and, like Dr. Howards says, commit, focus, work hard, seek feedback and strategize accordingly.

Students must have a clear understanding of the goals they want to achieve. What people desire or envision for themselves will give birth to their goals. As a student, you must ask yourself, "What is it that I want to accomplish?" Not having a clear understanding of what you want to achieve in life is like driving your car without first knowing where you are going; it will get you nowhere — a total waste of time and gas. For example, if you are planning to pursue a career in the medical field, then you know that you need to

Nurturing Your Intelligences

1. Have clear goals
2. Believe in yourself
3. Commit
4. Focus
5. Work hard
6. Seek feedback
7. Strategize

enroll and do well in rigorous science and math courses such as chemistry and pre-calculus. Clear goals regarding your future will allow you to make good decisions today.

Believing in your potential to learn is as important as setting clear goals. I always tell students that belief is to academic success what fuel is to a car engine. No matter how powerful a car engine is, without fuel it cannot go anywhere. Your belief will fuel your potential to learn and become more intelligent. Your level of belief will greatly influence your level of academic success.

Students can nurture their intelligences (or increase their ability to learn) when they demonstrate a high level of commitment. People who commit have strongly believe that what they want to accomplish is so good that it is worth their effort. When students are committed, their actions will demonstrate their determination to stay the course. A few days ago, I asked a 17-year old high school student who attended one of my college-bound student seminars, "Are you planning to enroll in college?" "Of course," he responded. "I am planning to be a Social Worker." Nevertheless, I was shocked and disappointed with his attitude during my seminar. The room was full of highly motivated students. All students, except him, were engaged in class and even the shyest of them found ways to participate. He did not seem to care and found funny and laughed at everything the students said. In my opinion, this student's actions during this seminar did not demonstrate commitment to achieve academic success and become a professional. His attitude not only did not allow him to learn but could also interfere with his journey to college and sabotage what could otherwise be great potential.

Focus can empower you to learn what you never thought you could. People who focus are involved in their work; they persist despite challenges and avoid distractions. They avoid diversions when engaged in activities that will lead to reaching their academic goals. For example, a student who wants to focus on his schoolwork will not hang out with friends, play video games or text while doing homework or studying for a test. This student will delay the gratification of socializing until the necessary task is complete. You need a lot of focus to write a quality essay or study for a physics test. Running away from distractions and finding the right time and place to comply with your school responsibilities is pivotal to becoming more intelligent.

Students who want to become more intelligent and excel in school know that they need to work hard. Nothing worth it in life, including knowledge, comes easy. Hard work, in my opinion, is one of the effective-effort components that leads to greater intelligence. People with a strong work ethic believe that work is honorable. Students who work hard are usually dependable, reliable and show initiative to acquire new knowledge in class. The students that teachers enjoy the most are not the ones that learning comes easy to them, but the ones that sweat learning new things. In strongly believe that bragging about acing a test with little effort is silly. Acing a test is admirable when it is the result of numerous hours of study.

Seeking and paying consideration to your teachers' feedback can accelerate your learning process and make you smarter. Feedback is the mechanism or process that allows people to improve their performance. In the academic world, feedback provides students information regarding what they are doing well and the areas they need to improve. For example, you cannot improve your writing skills by just writing. Before you turn in your essay, someone should read it to see if you made grammatical mistakes or if the main idea is not clearly stated. That person will help you improve the quality of your paper. I always tell students that their performance on previous assignments and tests is a great source of feedback. You cannot improve unless you know what to improve. For example, if you earned a D on your last Biology test, use that test to see the questions that you missed and find out why you got them wrong. What students learn from their mistakes will definitely make them smarter.

Strategizing is vital to achieving your academic goals. People in general strategize to bring about a desired future, reach a goal or solve a problem. Students who strategize decide which steps to take in order to fulfil their school responsibilities. What you learn from your teacher's feedback or your performance on previous assignments or tests will help you to come up with good strategies. You must ask yourself, "Based on the feedback that I received, what can I do differently to have a better outcome?" If you are regularly tardy to school, you must decide which strategies can help you be on time. If you scored lower than a 22 (ACT Benchmark) on the math portion of the ACT, you must decide what to do to improve that score. A good strategy to avoid being tardy, is going to bed earlier so you can have at least eight hours of sleep. I good strategy to increase your ACT math score is enrolling in a high-quality prep-course and taking the test again.

According to Sal Khan, founder the online Khan Academy, students must change the way they think about learning. In his own words, "… intelligence is not fixed and the best way we grow our intelligence is to embrace tasks where we might struggle and fail." You must persist and continue in spite of struggles and

> "… intelligence is not fixed and the best way we grow our intelligence is to embrace tasks where we might struggle and fail."

failures. Like stated before, failure is not final.

In conclusion, the amount of effort that you put into learning is more powerful that the genes you inherit from your parents. As I stated at the beginning of this competency, an apple seed cannot become an apple tree without good soil, water and light. Nature gave the seed the potential but nurturing allowed it to become a tree. Increase and strengthen the neurological connections in your brain cells to become more intelligent. If you have clear goals, believe in yourself, commit, work hard, focus, seek feedback and strategize accordingly, then nothing will stop you from experiencing what you have envisioned for yourself.

Competency # 8

EMBRACING THEMSELVES

Students embrace themselves and pursue physical, emotional and social health.

"Every school day I walk through the crowded and very diverse hallways of West Aurora High School. I see the typical 'popular people' yelling across the hall. I also see all of the other usual high school cliques, the 'Goths,' the 'Weirdoes,' and then those who struggle to fit in anywhere. I also see the ones who do not have many friends. In the past, I used to struggle making friends too. All that I lacked was someone to give me a little more self-confidence. It was not until now, my junior year, when I actually have an idea of who I am. I am, for the most part, comfortable with the student, neighbor, friend, brother, son, cousin, grandson, nephew, and overall person who I am."

- Nicolas Barrios

"In order to grow and succeed as a person, we need to have a strong and sturdy foundation, one that we can build on. The problem is that we, as students living in stressful environments with many worries and responsibilities, tend to put ourselves last when it should be our priority. Abraham Maslow once said, 'What a man can be, he must be. This need we call self-actualization.' This means that every person should strive to reach their potential in life and be the best they can be. Maslow, the American psychologist who created the hierarchy of needs, believed that every person needed to fulfill their basic needs in order to become self-actualized." - Evelyn Ganchuz

During my student leadership seminars, I always plead with participants to love, respect and take good care of themselves. Not long ago, I heard one high school student publicly say, "I hate everything about myself! I don't' like the way I am and I cannot stand looking at myself in the mirror. " We were all in shock! An atmosphere of negativity saturated the environment. What that student did not understand

It is very hard to embrace people who do not embrace themselves. People in general are likely to value you as much as you value yourself.

is that it is very hard to embrace people who do not embrace themselves. People in general are likely to value you as much as you value yourself. Know what your unique and personal attributes are and start looking at those as assets to your success. That is why embracing ourselves and doing whatever it takes to meet our emotional, social and physical needs is one of the twelve competencies that will prevent you from becoming a college casualty, that is, a student who never graduates college or graduates with degrees that are not in demand and/or with unbearable amounts of debts.

Every person in this world is a unique individual. Each one of us was born with a composition of physical characteristics, a blend of temperaments and a combination of intelligences. Physically, when compared to the norm, or average, some people are tall and others are short. Some basketball players, for example, are seven feet tall while a gymnast can be as short as four feet and eleven inches. Some people are extremely thin, no matter how much they eat. Others, including myself, are twenty-plus pounds overweight, gaining weight just by looking at food. I am just kidding!

> Every person in this world is a unique individual. Each one of us was born with a composition of physical characteristics, a blend of temperaments and a combination of intelligences.

We have different skin colors, hair texture and color of eyes. The point is that each one of us is unique with our own composition of inherited physical traits.

A negative attitude towards yourself can hurt your ability to achieve academic success. For example, students who dislike themselves elude attention. They are likely to avoid the front seats in class, which in my opinion are the best ones to learn and establish positive connections with your teachers. They evade participating in class, joining study groups or giving class presentations. Failure to participate in activities like this can have a negative impact in their grades and lower their GPA. Low self-esteem, or lack of appreciation for who you are physically, can lead to isolation and isolation can lead to failure. The time will come in which you will need your peers' collaboration and

According to the famous Gautama Buddha, "You can search throughout the entire universe for someone who is more deserving of your love ... You, yourself, as much as anybody in the entire universe, deserve your love and affection."

your teachers' support to achieve your academic and career goals. According to the famous Gautama Buddha, "You can search throughout the entire universe for someone who is more deserving of your love and affection than you are yourself, and that person is not to be found anywhere. You, yourself, as much as anybody in the entire universe, deserve your love and affection."

I inherited from my parents both Caucasian and Negro physical traits. Because I am a light-skinned black woman with an afro, people intrigued by my appearance usually ask me, "What is your race?" When I was a little girl, my peers used to make fun of my hair. Most of my relatives were disappointed with the fact that I was born with what they called "bad hair." I grew up with the habit of changing my hair appearance to fit in. At the age of twenty-one, I realized how ignorant and hurtful this kind of thinking was. I stopped relaxing my hair and embraced the composition of my physical features. I was able to experience the peace and contentment that comes from being comfortable in my own skin. I learned to like myself! Now these physical attributes are an asset.

Did you know that genetic factors regulate 50% of our personality? A big component of our personality is our innate temperament, which is the combination of emotional and mental genetic predispositions. Psychology scholars in ancient times thought that the level and combination of body fluids determined a person's temperament. They believed that the four basic temperaments were sanguine, phlegmatic, choleric and melancholic. Although we believe that genes, not body fluids, regulate our innate temperament, we still use this ancient theory to understand and describe human behavior and the differences among people.

According to this theory, sanguine people are extroverts, tend to be optimistic and can make new friends easily. In today's classrooms, students whose primary temperament is sanguine can struggle with following through on tasks and be chronically late or forgetful.

Choleric people are task-oriented, good at planning and focused on getting a job done. Student with choleric traits can be too ambitious, strong-willed and controlling. I see many of these traits in my children and myself. Imagine that household!

Folks with significant melancholic traits are introverted, cautious and concerned with people's pain or suffering. Melancholic students might be too hard on themselves when they do not meet their own standards and prefer to work independently because they are not inherently sociable.

This theory states that phlegmatic people are private, have rich inner lives and are usually content with themselves. Peers with phlegmatic temperament traits appear somewhat ponderous or clumsy and their speech tends to be slow or appear hesitant.

We must keep in mind that all of us have an exceptional blend of these four temperaments and that is what makes us so unique. I must ask you now, what is your temperate blend? Do you consider yourself a strong sanguine or mainly choleric? Learning and embracing your temperament, or unique blend of emotional and mental genetic predispositions, as well as your unique composition of physical trait, will empower you to achieve your academic and career goals. I, personally, learned to see my choleric-sanguine temperament traits as a plus in my career.

Four Temperaments

1. Sanguine
2. Choleric
3. Phlegmatic
4. Melancholic

As you can see, every type of temperament has its strengths or positives and its weaknesses or negatives; however, as we have discussed in this book, with effective effort we can improve or develop any area of our lives. For example, Beatrice is a freshman student with strong sanguine traits. Her peers know her as a very friendly extrovert who struggles following through her academic tasks. She can easily get distracted and forget about her classroom assignments. After her mom got an email from her History teacher saying that Beatrice did not turn in her homework assignment on time, her mom said to Beatrice, "I am sorry honey, but your tendency to be easily distracted and forgetful will not be an excuse for not complying with your responsibilities. We will set specific goals and put in place some good strategies to help you focus, avoid disruptions and learn responsibility. Responsibility is key to achieving your academic goals." Robert, on the other hand, is a senior student with very strong melancholic traits. His peers know him as a very kind introvert who does not enjoy working with others. When Robert's chemistry teacher assigned him to work with a group of his peers on a project, his teacher who knows him really well said to him, "Robert, I know that you prefer to work independently, however, you must also learn how to be a successful team member. Put some effort into this because today's job market needs people who can effectively work with others in pursue of common goals."

We are also born with a unique combination of intelligences. According to Dr. Howard Gardner, a well-known psychologist and author of the Multiple Intelligence theory, there are nine types of intelligences - logical, linguistic, musical, kinesthetic, inter-personal, intra-personal, spatial, naturalistic and existential. People with logical (or mathematical) intelligence are "number/reasoning smart." Students with lots of this intelligence can easily calculate, hypothesize and carry out mathematical algorithms.

Linguistic Intelligence makes people "word smart." This intelligence gives students the ability to think in words and skillfully use language to express and appreciate complex meanings.

Musical intelligence allows people to be "musically smart." Students born with this intelligence have the capacity to discern pitch, rhythm and tone and can effortlessly create or reproduce music.

People with kinesthetic (or bodily) intelligence are "body smart." They have the capacity to easily manipulate objects and use a variety of physical skills. Students with this intelligence have a sense of timing and the perfection of skills through mind–body union.

People with inter-personal intelligence, also known as "people smart," have the ability to interact with others effectively. Students with this intelligence are good communicators and seem to understand others' feelings and motives.

Intra-personal intelligence makes people "self-smart." Individuals with this type of intelligence have the capacity to understand themselves, including their thoughts and feelings. Students with this intelligence use their self-awareness to plan and monitor their personal lives.

People with spatial intelligence are "picture smart." Spatial intelligence gives humans the ability to think in three dimensions. Students with lots of spatial intelligence have active imagination and can analyze and manipulate objects mentally.

Naturalist intelligence allows people to be "nature smart." This intelligence gives humans the ability to discriminate among living and non-living things. Students with this type of intelligence can easily see the features and characteristics of elements in the natural world such as animals, plants, rocks, etc. and all kinds of objects such as cars, types of materials, fabric textures, etc.

Although we do not know too much about the existential Intelligence, we believe that it can give people the sensitivity and capacity to tackle deep questions about human existence. Students with this type with intelligence are likely to think and enthusiastically engage in conversation about the meaning of life, death and after life.

Spend some time thinking about yourself. Are you mostly word-smart, number-smart or people-smart? You might be a blend of self-smart, music-smart with a bit of existential intelligence. Whatever you are, embrace it! Now, you must also do whatever it takes to excel in the areas that you are already strong and make a significant effort to improve in the areas you might be weak, or not that strong.

Nine Types of Intelligences

1. Logic
2. Linguistic
3. Musical
4. Kinesthetic
5. Inter-personal
6. Intra-personal
7. Spatial
8. Naturalistic
9. Existential

For example, you might be music-smart. Your friends know that you are the best trumpet player in your school band. On the other hand, you are not body-smart. Your best friends also know that you are not good in any sport. In fact, you even hate your PE (Physical Education) class! Then, what are you going to do? Are you going to hurt you GPA by failing you PE class? You already know that through effective effort (determination, focus, hard work, etc.) you can learn whatever you want to learn, even any sport. At the end, you might not qualify to join any of your school's sport teams but you will definitely ace your PE class.

You might be more word-smart than number-smart. Is that a reason to Ace you English Language Arts class and fail your Algebra class? No! If you are good with words, I challenge you to become the best writer in your class or school. At the same time, if you struggle with math, I am asking you to do whatever it takes to pass your Algebra class with at least a B and then, put the necessary effort to meet with success the rest of your math requirements for high school graduation.

Embracing yourself will also require learning how to meet your basic physical, emotional and social needs. Quality air, a nutritious diet, plenty of exercise and plenty of sleep are some of your basic physical needs. Good quality of air will promote robust mental functioning and will impede the spread of airborne diseases. A nutritious diet will help you uphold total health and deter many illnesses. Like it or not, plenty of daily exercise will help you enjoy optimal physical development and a feeling of well-being. Among many other things, enough sleep will prolong your life and improve your memory. When I was a math teacher, I remember having students who did not have the energy to stay focused because they were hungry. They had the bad habit of coming to school without breakfast. Others watched TV or played video games way over their

As you can see, taking care of your physical needs is imperative to excel in school. Do not just take care of yourself for the sake of your education and success; take care of yourself because you are worth the effort!

recommended sleeping time. They would doze out in class and miss class instruction. Being sleepy or hungry can likely lead to academic failure. As you can see, taking care of your physical needs is imperative to excel in school. Do not just take care of yourself for the sake of your education and success; take care of yourself because you are worth the effort! You deserve a quality life, and you must provide for yourself the foundation to live that.

You must also be aware of your emotional needs. These needs include affection, discipline, a sense of belonging and encouragement. Affection is simply love. Experiencing love is essential in life in its many forms. Discipline, although not always sought, can empower you to live a balanced and healthy life. We, as humans, also need to experience a sense of belonging. Knowing that we are part of a family, and not a simple accident in life, creates enormous contentment. Each one of us also needs encouragement. Encouragement helps us believe that we can overcome challenges in life. Emotions are strong! They can build you up or bring you down. I know that it is very difficult for students to engage in school activities when they are sad, afraid or anxious.

> Emotions are strong! They can build you up or bring you down. ... Students are in a better position to reach their potential in life when they are able to understand and meet their emotional needs.

Students are in a better position to reach their potential in life when they are able to understand and meet their emotional needs.

As social beings, none of us can live in isolation. We have been "wired" to be part of a community. That is why we must be aware of our social needs, which include effective communication, acceptance, significant relationships, and meaningful involvement. We communicate effectively when we, verbally and non-verbally, express our ideas and feelings clearly. This is essential not only to be inclusive of others but also to set healthy boundaries. We all need to experience acceptance, not only by our parents, siblings and extended family members but also by our peers. A healthy social life also requires meaningful relationships with non-family members. Although our families play an important social role in our lives, these relationships alone do not suffice our social needs. We need friends, people who we enjoy being with and can relate to, one way or another. As social beings, we also need to be involved in such a way that we can make significant contributions in our social circles. In other words, if we are absent we want others to miss us. The students who usually performed very well in my advanced math courses were those who were comfortable in my class and contributed to a positive classroom experience. They sought help either from me or from their classmates every time they needed to. School was their second home and many of their peers were like family. A student that I was advising few months ago said to me, "I hate coming to school." Referring to his classmates he added, "I cannot wait until I never see anyone of them again!" This kind of attitude precludes students from meeting some of their social basic needs. A significant aspect of your success in life will depend on your social well-being, which involves building healthy relationships. Students have a better chance to achieve academic success when they can successfully recognize and meet their social needs. I do not have the words to stress enough

> A significant aspect of your success in life will depend on your social well-being, which involves building healthy relationships. Students have a better chance to achieve academic success when they can successfully recognize and meet their social needs.

the importance of embracing yourself. You must accept and see as an asset your unique composition of physical traits, blend of temperaments and combination of intelligences. To succeed academically and reach your career goals you must also be aware and able to meet your physical, emotional and social needs. You, better than anyone else, is willing and able to take care of yourself. As I stated before, people will like you at the level that you like yourself. There is no one in this world like you. Take advantage of it.

Competency # 9

ESTABLISHING GOALS AND MANAGING TIME

Students establish short and long-term goals and manage their time wisely.

"Throughout time, there have been individuals with great minds. Minds that helped themselves and the world be extremely successful. One of these great minds was George Washington, the first President of the United States. Others like Mahatma Gandhi and Martin Luther King Jr., who fought for human rights with no violence. However, even these great people needed to plan for success just like students who expect excellence and success in their own future should."

- Armando J. Davila

Have you ever heard the expression, "Whoever does not plan is planning to fail?" I am sure that you, like many other American students, have more things to do than hours in the day. That was not the case when I was growing up. There were no extra-curricular activities for high school students. At that time in Puerto Rico, students did not have part time jobs. The few jobs available were for adults. My job was to go to school, do homework, and help around the house. Today, the life of a high school American student is very different. Not long ago, in one of my student leadership seminars, I asked the students, "Is there any one of you who would like to share what a normal school day is for you?" I asked that question as an icebreaker to teach students how to manage their time in the most effective manner. Anxious to respond, George, a very smart and extroverted student said, "I wake up every morning at 6:00AM to go to school. Every day after school, I have football practice. After my practice, I go to work. After work, I do homework or study for any test. I usually go to bed like at 12:00 AM to be up again at 6:00." It sounded like a normal day to most of them but not to me. Then I thought to myself, "Can this kind of daily schedule help (or impede) this young man reach his purpose in life?"

As an academic advisor and coach, I know that a well-planned and balanced life is pivotal for students reaching their maximum (not partial) potential in life. It is for this reason that I believe that - the ability to set goals and manage time wisely must be one of the twelve competencies to avoid becoming a college casualty, one more student in the United Sates who never graduates, graduates with a degree that is not in demand or graduates with a surmountable amount of debts.

> As an academic advisor and coach, I know that a well-planned and balanced life is pivotal for students reaching their maximum (not partial) potential in life.

Let us start with goals. Why are goals so important? Most successful people believe that goals are necessary to move ahead in life, living meaningful and productive lives. Goals direct our actions and provide us with a sense of purpose. Goals are so powerful that they even shape our attitudes towards things, people and circumstances. There are two types of goals, short and long-term. Let me start with the long-term goals.

Ask yourself, "Where do I want to be in five years from now? Do you want to be a high school or a college graduate? How much money do you want to be making? For example, if you are in 11th grade (high school junior), there is a lot that you can accomplish in five years. You could

> Goals direct our actions and provide us with a sense of purpose. Goals are so powerful that they even shape our attitudes towards things, people and circumstances.

graduate high school, enroll in college and earn a 4-year college degree. If you are 16 years old now, by then, you will be 21 years old. Could you imagine?

In a recent psychological study conducted by Alberta School of Business, researchers made a mind-blowing discovery – once we set a long-term goal, our subconscious mind will never "erase" it. No matter where we live, what we do and how old we are, our subconscious will continue actively searching for ways to achieve those long-term goals. In my opinion, you can cultivate this subconscious drive to achieve those long-term goals by envisioning the details of your future.

At the age of 16, I knew that at the age of twenty-one, I had to make sufficient money and be independent enough to get myself out of the misery I grew up in. I was desperate! My father was an alcoholic and a very violent man. My mother put up with that because she did not make enough money to support my three siblings and me. I did not want to be like my mother, putting up with abuse for her lack of ability to stand up on her own. I knew that a college degree was the door to opportunities for a better life. My long-term goal was to earn a 4-year college degree before I turned 21. I made it! By the age of 21, I was as a high school math teacher in one of the most prestigious private schools in Puerto Rico, *El Colegio Puertorriqueño de Niñas*.

Throughout the years working with high school students, I have encountered too many who are clueless regarding what they want in life. They cannot see beyond their high school graduation and some of them not even that. One student in particular once said to me, "I just live one day at a time. I will deal with things as they come." Not long ago, without any shame or concern, a high school senior expressed, "I am worry-free. As long as I have my parents, I will be ok! My parents will provide me with anything I need." This kind of attitude in life does not lead to a life with a purpose; therefore, does not require any kind of goals.

On the other hand, I have encountered students who have a clear picture, or a vision, of who they want to be in five or more years from now. Juan, a senior high student who I personally admire a lot, shared with me that he wanted to be a medical doctor. Since I am not personally drawn to medical-related careers, I asked him, "Are you sure about that? You will have to deal with sicknesses, death and all that kind of stuff." In response to my questions he said, "I am fascinated with the human body, especially the brain. Hopefully, after I graduate as a medical doctor, which will take me eight years, I will continue to become an anesthesiologist." His vision and determination reminded me of myself when I first came to this country. Coming to the United States was crossing a frontier to me, and like Juan, I had a vision of whom I wanted to be in this great country.

While long-term goals can be meaningful and gratifying, they are usually far off in your future. By experience, I know that it can be challenging to maintain a positive attitude and stay focused on reaching them. To prevent getting off track, you must determine short-term goals. It is like breaking your long-term goal into smaller goals. Short-term goals are as important as long-term goals because only individuals who reach these "smaller" goals are able to reach the "big" ones. If you are just starting high school, you could ask yourself, "What goals must I establish this semester, this year, etc. to be in the position I need to be when I graduate high school?" Since I was in 9th grade, I learned that my parents did not have the financial resources to pay for my college education. By then I knew that doing my homework every day and acing every test would lead to a high GPA. A high GPA was, and still is, the door that leads to the best universities and plenty of free-money - not student loans, but grants and scholarships. I graduated from the University of Puerto Rico, the best university in my country. I never paid a penny. On the contrary, they paid me!

Going back to Juan, since he started high school he enrolled in the "right" math and science classes. In ninth grade, he took Honors Geometry so he could take AP Calculus in his senior year. He took Biology, Chemistry and Physics, so he could take AP Environmental Science in his senior year. After long hours of preparation, he earned a 30 Composite score on the ACT, which placed him on a 95th national percentile rank. As you can see, Juan's big goal of getting a "free ride" into a good pre-med program is the result of many smaller ones including reaching a high GPA and earning a high ACT score.

Now, let us move into managing your time. It is extremely difficult for anyone to reach short or long-term goals without good time-management skills. You have heard the expression, "time is money," more true in the United States than in any other part in the world. Unfortunately, time is continually passing but we are not continually making money, right? You can have all the time you want (or need); but never accomplish anything in life. How you manage your time, and what you do with it, is crucial to reaching your academic and career goals. Out of the many reasons why time-management is so crucial in our lives, I would like to mention the ones that I consider more relevant to academic success.

First, time goes fast, is limited and non-reversible. Once is gone you cannot get it back. That is why to excel in school and reach your career goals you must take control and make the most of your time. Taking control of your time will help you stay focused on what you need to do and focus will fuel the momentum you need to be efficient. I know too many people who wished they could go back in time. Their past waste of time led them to a present life of scarcity.

Second, decision-making requires time. As a student, you will often face many choices to choose from at the same time. Decisions made under the pressure of time are usually poor decisions. Good time-management skills will give you the time you need to determine which choices are the best to make. Choosing which college to apply to and which degree to pursue, for example, requires time to think. Rushing through decisions like this can lead to situations you might regret for a long time.

Third, time-management leads to success. Students with good time-management skills always accomplish more than those who do not because they take control of their lives rather than follow the flow of others. Waste of time is the number one reason why some students take up to ten years to complete a 4-year college degree and others never graduate. Good use of time empowers students to achieve higher academic success, gain meaningful experiences and move up sooner in life.

Fourth, poor time-management skills leads to stress. Did you know that one of the main causes of stress in life is the lack of time or feeling rushed all the time? With good time-management skills, you will know how much time you have available and how long each academic task will take. This will give you more breathing room and reduce the feeling of being rushed. Knowing how to manage your time will empower you to make informed decisions about what other responsibilities you can afford to take on. This is especially important to those students with multiple talents and skills who are both ambitious and seriously driven. My daughter, Deborah, was infamous in school for always having a full plate. In her fourth year of a five-year Architecture program, she was taking over 24 credits while maintaining a full time job. There is only so much one person can do, and that was the first year that she ever failed a class. In her own words, "Mom, I admit that I took on too much responsibilities."

Fifth, time management skills will help you relax and enjoy life. We all need some free time to relax and unwind but, unfortunately, many students do not get enough free time because they are too busy trying to keep up with their daily school assignments and extra-curricular activities. Some, like George, must also go to work. By implementing good time-management skills, you will be able to get more things done in a shorter period, leading to extra time to relax or enjoy life.

Sixth, time management skills can defeat procrastination. People with good time- management skills can fight or are immune to procrastination. According to Wayne Gretzky, "Procrastination is one of the most common and deadliest of diseases and its toll on success and happiness is heavy." As a student, procrastination will not only steal your time but it will also make easy things hard and hard things harder. Time-management skills will help you develop the discipline you will need during your entire academic career and later on in life. In my role as an academic advisor or coach, let me provide you with some advice regarding setting goals and managing your time.

Advice # 1: Make measurable goals. One of the differences between a dream and a goal is that you cannot measure a dream but you can measure the achievement of a goal. When you establish a goal, you must not only state the what, but also the when and the how. For example, I would like to lose some weight is more like a dream that a goal. To be a goal it must sound like, "I will work out 4 times a week and limit my bread intake to two times a week; and by December 31, 2015, I will weigh twenty pounds less." "I want to earn a college degree," is a noble dream or desire. On the other hand, "In four years from now, I will be graduating from Saint Augustine College with a degree in Respiratory Therapy." Thinking of those goals is great, but putting them in writing is even better. It mind sound a bit crazy, but a year after I enrolled in my doctoral program, I used the software Publisher to create and post on the wall a fake diploma that included my name, degree, date of graduation and the name and logo of my university. Seeing the fake diploma posted on the wall kept me focused. Once you have that specific goal in mind, find a way to put it in front of you. Write it down in a journal at minimum.

Advice # 2: Always be realistic. Setting goals that are beyond your reach might lead to disappointment. Unmet expectations lead to frustration. For example, if you have struggled with math throughout your high school years, do not set a career goal that requires a lot of mathematics. "Even though that I hate math, I am planning to become an electrical engineer," one student in particular said to me.

"I need to dream high," he said. "That is a nice dream but an unrealistic goal," I replied. "You must consider a career that matches with your strengths, not weaknesses." The classes you enjoy and excel in now as a high school student are a strong indication of what you ought to pursue.

Advice # 3: Plan for the unexpected; life is full of twist and turns. When I have to fly somewhere, I always leave my house with plenty of time in case I have a flat tire, a car dysfunction or the traffic slows down due to an accident. I do not want to miss my flight, no matter what. In case the unexpected happens, you will abort Plan A and go for Plan B. For example, private universities are significantly more expensive than the public ones. Earning an Associate degree (the first two years of a 4-year college degree) at a close-to-home community college is a lot cheaper than taking those same courses at a far-from-home 4-year college campus. Therefore, if you submit your college application to several universities (even the community college close to home) you will be able to start your college education, even if you did not get the amount of financial aid you expected.

Advice # 4: Run your race with patience. Reaching goals, especially the long-term ones, requires time. You cannot have the attitude of a small child in a long road trip. "Are we there yet?" is what my five-year old grandchild continuously asks when I take him for a long car ride. He has a hard time enjoying the ride. Students who are planning to earn a college degree must learn to enjoy the journey that will take them to their final destination. Make the best out of every class you take because the time will come where you will wish to be a student again.

Advice # 5: Celebrate every success. Sometimes we live our lives complaining about everything. Some people are so negative that they can only see the bad side of things. This negativity is extremely contagious! Make a big deal about any academic success you experience. Celebrate events that help you or get you closer to achieving your goals. You celebrate by stopping everything you are doing to meditate on and enjoy your success. Smile, tell someone and thank anyone who had something to do with your accomplishment. Celebration will provide you with the positive energy you will need to continue your journey and reach your goals.

Time Management Strategies

1. Make measurable goals
2. Be realistic
3. Plan for the unexpected
4. Run your race with patience
5. Celebrate every success

As you can see, setting long-term goals will give you purpose and direction. Setting and achieving short-term goals will help you reach your purpose in life. Nevertheless, good time management skills will allow you to achieve those goals. Your daily activities, in what and how you spend your time speak about your priorities in life. Plan your life based on goals not dreams, always be realistic and plan for the unexpected. Walk your academic journey with patience and celebrate success. Your goals and the way you spend your time will determine the level of success you will experience in life.

Competency # 10

REACHING FINANCIAL LITERACY

Students plan and manage their financial resources wisely.

"Money is only one word with two syllables but it is what drives us as a society and makes the world go around. Some even say it talks, and you could claim that it walks and runs considering how long it remains within your account. Money is an item that can be shrouded as a virtue as well as a fault. It can open doors wide open, or close them shut completely. College is no exception to this. Thousands of students decide to go further during their high school careers. They are willing to spend more sleepless nights and longer mornings in order to achieve something greater in their education, but they simply cannot. Why? They do not have a strong financial base. This cannot continue happening! Students with great potential cannot become casualties even before going through the doors of a University."
- Christopher Rodriguez

I was surprised to learn that according to the NAEP (National Assessment of Educational Progress) 2012 Economic test report, only 43% of 12th grade students demonstrated knowledge regarding today's economy and the ability to use that knowledge in real-life situations. That means that the majority of high school graduates lack financial literacy. What concerns me even more is that this economic illiteracy is happening when the cost of living has skyrocketed and the cost of earning a college degree is way above what most Americans can afford. Experts in economy are reporting that rising prices for food, utilities, health insurance, and gasoline is leaving most American families with less money to save or spend in wants. The U.S. Department of Education reported that since 2001, the cost of a college public education increased by 40%.

> ... since 2001, the cost of a college public education increased by 40%. For most Americans, the pursuit of a post-secondary education or college degree is a luxury that they can no longer afford.

For most Americans, the pursuit of a post-secondary education or college degree is a luxury that they can no longer afford. That is why I consider that, the ability to understand, plan and manage their financial resources wisely, should be one of the twelve competencies for students to avoid becoming college casualties, which means, dropping out of college, earning degrees that are not in demand or graduating with unbearable debts.

There are several reasons, in my opinion, for the lack of financial literacy among so many young people. First, many high school students do not know how to manage money simply because they never had the opportunity to learn. I believe that all students have the ability to reach financial literacy and be money-smart. Nevertheless, very few teenagers have someone willing and able to teach them the knowledge and skills they need to do so. Most of the parents that participate in my academies, believe that they protect their children when they keep them away from money related issues. Students see both their parents faithfully going to work every day, sometimes having more than one job or working extra hours, just to make ends meet. Parents do not share with their children their financial challenges and strategies to overcome those challenges because they do not want their children to worry. They only want their kids to focus in their education. I have heard numerous parents say, "I do not want my children to be concerned about money. My job is to work as hard as I can to meet my children's needs and their job is to study as hard as they can to earn a college degree." For example, I have not yet met a high school student who knows how much money their parents make or how much money they spend in food monthly. They do not know how much utilities are or what an interest rate is on a mortgage. Most students are not aware of how much more their parents are paying when they include their children in their car

Reasons for Financial Illiteracy

1. Parents do not talk to their children about finances because they do not want their children to worry.
2. Money is no longer tangible- How do you show a child that there is no more money.
3. We live in a spending culture. "Whatever we like we want: and we want it now!"

and/or health insurance policies. Children become adults clueless of the amount of money they will need to maintain their accustomed standard of living.

The second reason that could be causing today's widespread economic illiteracy is that money is no longer tangible. When I was growing up in Puerto Rico, my parents paid everything in cash. We could see and touch bills and coins. We did not have credit or debit cards or ATM machines. With a little peek into my mom's wallet, I could see if she could pay for what I was getting ready to ask for. Today, most young people do not have a clear understanding of their families' daily financial transactions. Not long ago, my 5-year old grandson Zacharie was insisting on me taking him to McDonalds. I was too tired to stop; so I said to him, "I don't have the money. Let's wait until we get home." He said, "Abuela [grandmother] look! There is an ATM machine there." He really thought that ATM machines existed to give money to anyone who needed it. Many children innocently think that ATM machines and plastic cards are all they require to get whatever they want or need in life. How do you show a child that there is no money? I leave that question for you to answer.

We live in a spending society. Our culture can create in many of us the need to acquire things than we do not really need. As a wise person once said, "Whatever we like we want; and we want it now!" This can be the third reason for so much financial illiteracy, especially among young people. Students who want to become money-smart or intelligent users of their financial resources must fight and overcome the need to have all they want or desire in life. I other words, we must control our need for immediate gratification. Natasha Munson, the CEO of Be Magic, Inc., a nonprofit organization dedicated to empowering single mothers and their children once said, "Money, like emotions, is something you must control to keep your life on the right track." As I said at the beginning, college degrees are expensive! Every penny that you do not spend in needless things is a penny you can spend on your education.

> Natasha Munson ... once said, "Money, like emotions, is something you must control to keep your life on the right track."

When I enrolled in college in 1972, the Financial Aid office qualified me to receive Pell Grant money because my parents could not afford to pay for my college education. We were poor indeed. Because my GPA was 4.0, I also received the Presidential Award. With all that money, I was able to pay tuition, fees, books and school supplies and still had some money left. Although college was far away from home, I decided to use public transportation instead of paying for student housing or buying a used car. It was hard! I exercised a lot of self-control to avoid the temptation of spending money on things that a normal teenage girl at that time would had loved to have. My wise financial decisions allowed me to earn, debt-free, a Bachelor's Degree in Mathematics in less than four years.

To increase your financial literacy or improve your money-management skills, I highly suggest that you consider and maybe implement the following strategies. First, find out how much money you would need to be financially independent, as simple as that. Just imagine that you were totally on your own and your parents (or any other relative) were not there to help you. How much money would you need per week, month and in a year to support yourself and maintain your current standard of living? Sit with your parents and learn how much money they spend in rent (or mortgage), electricity and gas, car payments, gasoline, car insurance, health insurance, and so on. I know that the list is long and this is not an easy task. However, the more you learn about the cost of living the better prepared you will be to plan and manage your future college financial life. The awesome part of this strategy is that it will also help you decide which college degrees can open doors to job opportunities that pay enough to maintain (or improve) the life style your grew up in. There are many college graduates making less money that their parents did when they were growing up. Living in your parents' basement, unemployed or making a minimum wage salary with a college degree is worst, in my opinion, than never earning a college degree. I can assure you that it is deeply depressing to live in poverty after years of college education.

Second, before making a final decision regarding which college or university you will attend, find out the total amount of money you will need to earn your degree. Students who attend public high schools might not know how to conduct this kind of analysis. High school students who attend public schools enjoy free classes and books. Students who qualify also enjoy free lunch and receive free transportation if needed. Once you graduate high school, things change drastically. You must pay tuition and fees for the courses you take. The books are usually extremely expensive. You will also pay for lunch and transportation. All of these expenses can add up to a significant amount of money.

Third and last, make a great effort to reach financial literacy. In other words, become a money-savvy student. Read books, take courses or learn from people who are experts in money management how to reach and maintain financial health. For example, put a price tag to anything you want to do. Do not launch yourself into things you cannot afford. Do not spend more money than you make. Save enough money to cover any emergency. Name every dollar because each one has a purpose! Avoid continuously living on the edge of a financial crisis because being broke all the time can lead to broken dreams.

Strategies for Reaching Financial Literacy

1. Find out how much money you would need to be financially independent.
2. Find out the total amount of money you will need to finance your college education.
3. Make a great effort to reach financial literacy. In other words, become a money-savvy student.

As you can see, I am very passionate about this topic. You might know that the main reason why I immigrated into the United States, leaving my country, culture and relatives behind was to improve the quality of my children's lives. As any other immigrant, I came to pursue the American Dream. However, as I said before, being broke can lead to broken dreams. The dream of living a qualify life requires sufficient and steady financial resources and for that - we must reach financial literacy.

Competency # 11

REACHING ASSESSMENT LITERACY

Students understand the purpose, format and administration of the standardized tests they take.

"Most students get very nervous before any test, especially if the test is very important. It is also true that we get even more anxious once we start thinking that we will fail. You can control this anxiety and these nerves by knowing that you will not fail. Why? You know that you prepared yourself well. That is why I believe that more important than anything else is knowing what will be on these tests. If you know what the test is testing, then you can prepare accordingly. When you are prepared, there is no reason for you to be afraid."
-Melissa Medellin

When I immigrated into the United States, one of the first things I learned was that assessment or testing is critical in the American culture. When I established myself in Miami, Florida, my sister Vilma said to me, "You must get your Florida Driver's License as soon as possible. Driving around without a valid license can get you into big trouble." "That is not a problem," I said to myself. "I am an experienced driver." For more than a decade, I drove motorcycles, cars and trucks through mountains and across rivers in Central America. Nevertheless, I was shocked when the person at the information desk said, "Ma'am, to get your Florida driver's license you will need to pass both a written and a driving test." I was almost offended; but reluctantly, prepared and passed both of them. Not long after that, to get my teaching certificate, I was required to take a whole battery of tests, even though I already had a BS in mathematics and a MS in Research, Measurement and Evaluation. I cannot even remember the amount of tests I had to pass to be in the position that I am in today. That is why I strongly consider that reaching assessment literacy must be one of the twelve competencies presented in this book. Students who are proficient test-takers can avoid becoming a college casualty; that is, one more student who drops out of college, earns a degree that is not in demand or graduates with enormous amounts of debts.

Students who are assessment literate understand not only the purpose and format, but also the administration process of every test they take. They know how to read and interpret their assessments' reports. They are also aware of the impact that their performance will have on their academic lives.

Experts in the field of academic and personal growth agree that assessment or testing is vital for reaching proficiency in any academic subject and attaining academic goals.

Teachers, school administrators, students and any organization that seeks to improve their standing, need to use assessments to measure their level of success regarding pre-established objectives. Experts in the field of academic and personal growth agree that assessment or testing is vital for reaching proficiency in any academic subject and attaining academic goals. Many institutions and businesses are subject to varying degrees of testing to qualify for certifications and awards.

I am sure that you, as a student, more than anyone else, know about assessments. Teachers are regularly testing students to see if they are attaining the knowledge and skills they need to pass the class, get the credit and graduate high school. Students take quizzes, end-of-unit tests and semester final exams. Your teachers design or select these classroom assessments and your performance in them will determine if you pass the class or not. Students, especially the ones who are determined to pursue a post-secondary education, pay a lot of attention to these assessments because at the end, their performance will determine their Grade Point Average (GPA). They know that a high GPA can open doors to many post-secondary education opportunities.

Students, even those in Kindergarten, are subject to standardized tests. Standardized tests are very different from classroom assessments because their design, administration, scoring and interpretation of scores are pre-established and standard for every student who participates in the process. For example, every year all students from third to eighth grade must take their own state's accountability standardized test. In the state of

Standardized tests are very different from classroom assessments because their design, administration, scoring and interpretation of scores are pre-established and standard for every student who participates in the process.

Illinois, students take the PARCC (Partnership for Assessment of Readiness for College and Careers). These standardized tests have two purposes - evaluate the performance of the states' schools and determine the college readiness of students. The basic question is, "Do American students have the knowledge and skills they need to pursue a college education or enter the workforce?" Because the PARCC is a standardized test, all students at a certain grade level, no matter where they live or the school they attend, will take the same test. The administration, scoring and analysis of the students' scores are the same all across the state of Illinois.

It is very important that high school students become aware that educational institutions, colleges and universities in particular, perceive standardized tests as a fair measure of student achievement because they permit a more reliable comparison of academic success across all test-takers. That is why most post-secondary institutions pay as much (if not more) attention to students' ACT or SAT scores than to their GPA. Not long ago a high school student said to me that not all high schools are the same. She transferred to a new school because her parents bought a house in a neighboring city. "In my old school, earning an A was not a big deal," she said to me. "Now I am lucky if I can keep up with my peers. I am working twice as hard to get at least a B. My GPA went down from a 3.9 to barely 2.9." The grades you earn in school will likely depend on the school you attend or the class you take. On the other hand, the scores you earn on a college entrance test will just depend on the knowledge and skills you have acquired throughout your academic life.

The questions that I ask myself is, "If standardized assessment are so important, why is it that so many students, especially African American and Hispanic students, do so poorly in most (if not all) of them?" For example, in the state of Illinois, 78% and 65% of 11th Asian and White students passed the math portion of the PSAE (Prairie State Assessment Exam), compared to 37% and 23% of Hispanics and Blacks. That means that approximately 63% and 73% of Hispanic and Black students, according to the state's accountability test, do not meet the state's mathematics proficiency standards.

Nationwide, most universities use the scores that students earn on the ACT to accept or deny admission; determine which courses (or career) students qualify to enroll; and, the amount of financial aid they will receive.

You might be surprised to see that more than 50% of Asian students met all the ACT college-readiness benchmarks while less than 50% of African American and Hispanic students did so. As you can see in this graph,

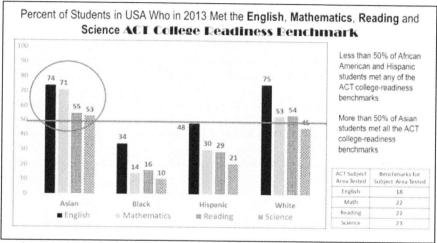

only 30% and 14% of Hispanic and Black students scored 22 (ACT Math Benchmark) or higher in the math portion of this important test. That means that 70% and 86% of Hispanics and African Americans are not ready to enroll in a college-level math course. As a Hispanic mother and mathematics teacher, I must say that these statistical facts saddens me deeply. There are several reasons that I believe are hurting students' performance on standardized tests.

Reason # 1

I believe that so much standardized testing is desensitizing students. By the time students are in high school, they have gone through the motions of these kinds of testing for a decade. For many students, it is simply one more test, that for whatever reason, they have to take. Every time that I advise or help a high school student, I must first know their standardized test scores in two key academic areas, reading and mathematics. I do this because there is always the possibility that their struggles in a History or Physics class is due to poor reading or math skills. So far, I have not met a student who, with certainty, knows the answer to these questions.

Reason # 2

Many students do not see the relevance of standardized tests. They know that   their performance on these tests does not affect their grades or GPA (Grade Point Average). Most students move to the next grade even if they perform poorly on these tests. In most states across the nation, including the state of Illinois, passing the state's accountability test is not a graduation requirement. One student in particular said to me, "Why should I care about a test that does not count? No matter how many answers I get wrong, I will able to graduate; so why should I bother?"

Reason # 3

Students can also perform poorly on standardized tests because the content, format and administration of a standardized test can be very different from their classroom teachers' tests. Teachers assess what they taught in class. They usually test what students should have learned in a chapter, unit or semester. On the other hand, standardized tests assess what students should have learned in years. Teacher-made exams might include different types of test items, similar to the questions students have been answering in quizzes or homework assignments. Standardized test items can be very different to what students deal with every day in class. Every alternative (or choice) in a multiple-choice item is designed to distract you from the right answer and many times you must choose not the right answer, but the best answer. Students usually have more than enough time to finish a classroom test, but need to rush through the questions when taking a standardized exam. The math portion of the ACT, for example, provides only 60 minutes to answer 60 problems. In the reading portion of the ACT, students are supposed to read four passages and answer 40 questions in less than 35 minutes.

Students are reading passages and solving math problems under enormous pressure of time.

Reason # 4

Many parents are assessment illiterate. They are clueless regarding the many tests that their children are now taking. They happily send their children to school and are only concerned about their kids' grades and behavior. In their minds, if their children pass to the next grade level it is because they are doing well in school. For them, graduating high school means that their children have the knowledge and skills they need to enroll college and earn a degree. Little do they know that, in the United States, we believe in "social promotion." Students pass to the next grade level even if they are performing below grade level. Did you know that an average 17-year old Hispanic or African American student performs at the same level as an average 13-year of white student? That is why seven to eight of every ten Hispanic and African American students are required to take prep-courses in college; wasting time, energy and money in courses that do not count towards their degree. I strongly believe that parents who are aware of the importance (and academic impact) of standardized assessments are more prepared to support their children's academic lives.

In order to overcome the challenges that standardized assessments present, I highly recommend you to embrace the idea that taking tests will always be a big component of your academic and career life. So instead of using your time and energy complaining about them, do whatever it takes to become an expert test-taker.

I suggest that before taking any test, you learn as much as you can about it. Among many other things you must know the content that is assessed, the types of items that are used, how much time do you have to complete the test, the passing or benchmark score, and if students are penalized for guessing. Let me give you an

Reasons that Hurt Students' Performance on Standardized Tests

1. Students are desensitizing by so mush standardized testing.
2. Students do not see the relevance of standardized tests.
3. The content, format and administration of standardized tests are very different from classroom assessments.
4. Parents are not aware of the importance (and academic impact) of standardized assessments in their children academic lives.

example of what I mean. If you are taking the ACT, you must know that this is a 100% multiple-choice standardized test used for college admission and financial aid purposes. The test has four sections – English, Reading, Mathematics and Science. While you have 45 minutes to answer 75 questions in the English section, which measures standard written English and rhetorical skills, you only have 35 minutes to answer 40 questions in the Reading section, which measures reading comprehension. These are just few of the many facts you must know about this test by memory.

You must also be aware that standardized tests also examine how well you take tests or your test-taking skills. The ACT, for example, is a test that gives you a significant probability of guessing or deducing the correct answer. If there are five choices (or alternatives), there is a 20% probability of guessing the right answer. That means that, if you do not know the right answer you must make an educated guess. Never leave it blank because there is no penalty for guessing. You can also employ the strategy of deduction. Knowing the choices that are not right increases your chances of choosing the right answer. Guessing and deducing are two of the many strategies that skillful test-takers use to do well on standardized tests.

Once you learn everything there is to learn about the test, invest a significant time studying and practicing. You must practice with the same intensity that you would to become good in any sport. You learn how to swim by swimming. You must get into the water and practice until you can speedily cross the pool without feeling that you are gasping for air. Practice makes perfection! It is disappointing when I see students preparing so little for tests such as the ACT, SAT and the ASVAB (Armed Services Vocational Aptitude Battery). They do not seem to be aware that their future academic lives and professional careers depend on their performance on these tests.

Be aware that the content tested in standardized tests and the types of questions asked might be very different to what they are used to seeing in class. There are students who think that going to school every day, participating in class, doing their homework and taking advance, honor or AP courses is enough. They are wrong! For example, a question that many students get wrong in the math portion of the ACT is "How many pages did you read from page 23 to the end of 30?" Most students would say seven because $30 - 23 = 7$. The answer is – eight pages. They forget to include page 30 (23, 24, 25, 26, 27, 28, 29 and 30). Another question frequently missed is, "How many times would you cut a string to get five equal parts? The answer is not five but four. As you can see, these types of questions are not common in a regular math class.

Be mindful that "gate keepers" will use your standardized test scores to make decisions regarding your academic future. For example, my granddaughter Gabriella was able to take Algebra 1 in 8th grade because she scored at Level 4 (above proficiency) in the math portion of Florida's standardized test. This will allow her to take AP Calculus in her senior year, a math course that opens doors to high-in-demand STEM (Science, Technology, Engineering and Math) careers. I am frustrated with the huge amount of students who take AP courses but do not pass the AP test. After so much hard work, they do not get any college credit. I have seen too many students who join the Arm Forces but their ASVAB test scores do not qualify them to enter into the military specialty of their choice.

The ability to perform well in any standardized tests is more important than many students think. Your performance on standardized tests will always have a huge impact in your academic and professional career. A smart test-taker is not something that you are, but something that you can become through effective effort. Assessment literacy is definitely one of the most important skills in a student's academic life and career path.

Ways for Improving Your Performance on Standardized Tests

1. Embrace the idea that taking tests will always be a big component or your academic and career life.

2. Before taking any test, learn as much as you can about it.

3. Be aware that standardized tests also examines how well you take tests or your test-taking skills.

4. Invest a significant time studying and practicing for every standardized test you have to take.

5. Be aware that the content tested in standardized tests, and the types of questions asked, might be very different to what they are used to seeing in class.

6. Be mindful that "gate keepers" will use your standardized test scores to make decisions regarding your academic future.

Dr. Lourdes Ferrer

Competency # 12

REACHING DIGITAL LITERACY

Students use technology to improve their academic achievement and reach their career goals.

"I believe that many of my same-age peers are not using technology to their benefit. I remember once, when I was a bit younger, that I stayed home twitting for hours. I really thought I had nothing to do. Nevertheless, the next day at school, I remembered that I had homework. I totally forgot about it! Most people have computers, different computer software, Smart phones, T.V., and internet access, and yet they are not using it to benefit themselves academically. Instead of using it for dumb and irrelevant purposes, we should use all these kinds of new technologies for more important reasons, such as meeting our academic needs." - Irving Espinoza

If you are in your twenties or younger you might not be aware of how different life is, when compared to thirty or more years ago. Since I am 59 years old, I am able to see how technology revolutionized the world we live in today. I still remember the first time we had a phone line in our house. My three siblings and I would fight over who would pick up the phone and say, "Hello!" We had one Black and White TV in the living room and listened to the latest music using an 8-track prayer. You might not know what I am talking about; but that is ok. Today I carry my android phone wherever I go to stay connected with my loved ones and the rest of the world. I download my favorite Salsa music from the internet; and instead of a typewriter machine, I use Microsoft Word to put my thoughts and feelings into writing.

> Technology is the new social equalizer because it has given all of us equal opportunity to acquire the knowledge we need to achieve our academic and professional goals.

Technology is the new social equalizer because it has given all of us equal opportunity to acquire the knowledge we need to achieve our academic and professional goals. On the other hand, technology presents challenges and leaves us vulnerable to dangers we have never seen before.

Making good use of our latest technology, or reaching digital literacy, in my opinion, is a competency students must acquire to avoid becoming a college casualty. In other words, one more student who drops out of college or graduates with a degree that is not in demand and/or overwhelming debts.

Before anything else, I would like to clarify what technology really means. Many people wrongly equate technology solely with computers. According to the Merriam Webster dictionary, technology is the use of knowledge or science to change or manipulate the environment. It includes tools, techniques, and sources of power to make work more efficient and productive, and life easier and more pleasant. In the Stone Age, for example, the latest technology was the discovery of fire, which provided humans a way to cook their food and generate heat and light. In the Bronze Age, the creation of the wheel was the technology that provided people greater ability to travel and communicate. In today's era, the creation of computers provided us with the ability to perform thinking processes more efficiently and faster than ever before. In my opinion, the three technological inventions that can provide students from all backgrounds an equal opportunity to achieve their academic goals are a word processor, access to the internet and participation in social media.

A word processor program does exactly what the name implies - it processes words. Compared to the typewriter, the most significant improvement is its ability to make changes to a document after written. You can go back and add, delete or edit a document without having to write the entire paper again, which I think is awesome! Word processors like Word, WordPerfect or AppleWorks provide features that allow you to customize the style of the text, change the page formatting and add headers, footers, and page numbers. When proofing your document, you can check your grammar with the Spelling & Grammar function. More importantly, you can see your document's readability, or level of reading difficulty. Long words or passive sentences, for example, can reduce the readability of your document. The lower the readability score, the more difficult it is for the reader to comprehend your writing. It is easier to read, "We did not go to the party because we did not purchase the tickets" than, "We would have gone to the party if we would have purchased the tickets." A Flesh Reading Ease score of 30 means that only

30% of people will easily understand your paper or essay. The average number of syllables per word and the average number of words per sentence will also determine your paper's grade level. A Flesh-Kinkaid Grade Level of 11 means that an average 11th grade student will be able to understand what you wrote. With Word (or any other word processor), you can "cleanly" write a paper that your teachers (and others) can understand. This skill will improve

By experience, I know that students who get the free-money are the ones who can express their thoughts and feelings in an error-free, easy to understand manner.

your grades and increase your GPA. You might also take into account that most scholarships sponsors require students to write an essay. By experience, I know that students who get the free-money (scholarships) are the ones who can express their thoughts and feelings in an error-free, easy to understand manner. Most readers will likely be offended by grammatical mistakes and lose interest in papers that they find hard to read.

Internet access is no longer a luxury but a necessity. The Internet is a virtual treasure of information. Any kind of information on any topic under the sun is available to anyone through the Internet. No wonder it is called the great equalizer! People can use it to find the best-qualified doctor to treat a family illness or the purpose and side effects of any medication. You can purchase any product or service after visiting different websites to compare prices and quality. We can learn anything about any country we want to visit including the culture, currency and best tourists' attractions. Even today, while writing this paper, I surfed the internet to learn about technology, the different kinds of word processors and even the benefits that the internet offers. As a student who is considering earning a college degree, the internet will give you access to all the information you need about any college degree and the institutions that offer them. You can electronically fill out the FAFSA, monitor the process, while looking for

> Internet access is no longer a luxury but a necessity. The Internet is a virtual treasure of information. Any kind of information on any topic under the sun is available to anyone through the Internet. No wonder it is called the great equalizer!

scholarships that can help you finance your education. Moreover, you can learn the places you could apply for a job after earning your degree. With internet access, a keyboard and a mouse you can plan your career path. Finally yet importantly, email is what I appreciate the most about the internet. I can receive and send instant electronic messages at no extra cost. Students can effectively communicate with teachers and send their classroom assignments as attachments. Through email, you can express yourself more extensively and effectively than ever a letter.

The third technological innovation that can accelerate and strengthen students' capacity to achieve their academic and career goals is the social media. According to the Merriam Webster Dictionary, social media are forms of electronic communications for users to create online communities to share information, ideas, personal messages, and other content. According to Nielsen's report, internet users

> The benefits of participating in social media went from simply connecting and sharing with people to building reputation, getting job opportunities, increasing business revenue and starting social movements.

spend more time in social media sites like Facebook, Instagram, LinkedIn and Twitter, than in any other type of websites. The benefits of participating in social media went from simply connecting and sharing with people to - building reputation, having access to job opportunities, increasing business revenue and starting social movements. For example, videos posted in social media are fueling an anti-police national sentiment and getting thousands of people protesting in the largest cities in the United States. Social media sites like LinkedIn allow individuals to post and update their education and work experience and potential employers around the world use it to meet their unique human resource demands. Personally, I use Facebook to communicate with the people I serve. I post messages, pictures and videos to share my ideas and invite people to participate in my events. As a student, you can use social media websites to create a positive image of yourself and strengthen your leadership skills. For example, you can let your peers know about the book you are using to improve your performance on the math portion of the ACT, a website they can visit or a course they can enroll to prepare for this test. After asking for permission, you can also post pictures that show you participating in a math or physics study group or attending a career conference. Most importantly, write about your experiences in a way that let others know how much you value education and your determination to achieve academic and life success. Remember that people will judge you based on what you post online. Be aware that people who can grant you a scholarship, an internship or a job opportunity might use the social media to a have a better sense of who you are.

After going over some of the benefits of today's technology, let me discuss some of the challenges and dangers that it presents. I am sure you have heard the adage, "A picture is worth a thousand words." Meaning that a single picture (or video) involving you, can deliver more information

> Whoever said, "Sticks and stones may break my bones, but words can never hurt me" was completely wrong. On the contrary, comments posted online can be weapons of character destruction.

about your character than a thousand words. While positive visuals can create a positive image of you, negative pictures or videos can ruin your reputation forever. Whoever said, "Sticks and stones may break my bones, but words can never hurt me" was completely wrong. On the contrary, comments posted online can be weapons of character destruction. What people say can hurt others emotionally, socially, academically and economically. Therefore, words as much as visuals have the power to create an image that opens doors or one that closes them forever.

Another danger that our technology presents is that predators (people who rob, victimize or exploit others for personal gain) are using the internet as their foremost way to reach their targets. They are cowards hiding behind their computer screens to commit their misdeeds. To name a few, people with the pedophilia psychiatric disorder use the social media to connect with children. Terrorist organizations use their websites and many social media venues to present their radical ideas and recruit new members. Identity thieves get key information about people to sell their identities in the cyberspace black market.

> Another danger that our technology presents is that predators (people who rob, victimize or exploit others for personal gain) are using the internet as their foremost way to reach their targets.

Experts in the field of mental health are reporting that computer video games, texting, social media websites, etc.

can be very addictive. Consumed by what they can experience in the cyber world, people of all ages are mentally abandoning their normal lives. People are becoming addicted to the sense of adventure and the pleasure of victory that video games provide. Did you know that the average adult looks at his smart phone 65 times a day? Go to any restaurant and you will see that the only time most customers are not touching their phones' screens is when they are busy eating. Teenagers in particular are texting so much that they are losing their ability to establish productive face-to-face conversation with others.

After discussing some of the advantages and dangers of today's technology, I would like to provide you with some advice. First, if you can, make sure that your computer has the software necessary to meet your academic needs. Because I am not a ""Mac" person, I suggest that you get the latest version of Microsoft Outlook, Power Point and Word. Once you learn how to use them, these three computer programs will allow you to create quality emails, documents and presentations.

Second, do not avoid the social media but take advantage of it. The social media is like a car; it can get you far but it can also get you into an accident. Therefore, you must learn how to "drive safely" in order to avoid tragedies. The social media that I advise is LinkedIn, Facebook and Twitter. Currently, these are the most popular in the professional world.

Third, do not allow people to take pictures or videos of you, or that includes you, without your permission. If the picture or video will portray you in a positive manner, by all means, jump in! If someone post a visual or a written comment that affects you, do not hesitate to boldly ask that person who posted it to delete it immediately. You must protect your image the same way you protect your life.

Fourth, be very careful with whom you connect with via internet. There are many mean and mentally sick people "hanging out" in the streets of the cyber world. Do not provide any kind of information to people you have not personally met. More than anything protect your address, social security number and driver's license number.

Fifth, do not think you are immune to cyber-addiction. All of us, in one time or another, can have a hard time letting go the cyber world because the internet can artificially meet many of our emotional and social needs. In the cyber world, we can have fun, feel loved and develop a sense of belonging, especially in vulnerable times. If you are going through hard times in life, seek the help you need from people you physically know and truly care about you.

Strategies Regarding the Use of Technology

1. Install in your computer the software you need to meet your academic needs.
2. Do not avoid the social media but take advantage of it.
3. Do not allow people to take pictures or videos of you without your permission.
4. Be careful with whom you connect with via internet.
5. Do not think you are immune to cyber-addiction.

In conclusion, I must say that I am glad I was not born in any of the previous eras. Among many other things, I love being able to fly to any part of the world, stay in touch with the people I love via phone, text or Skype, and get all the information I need via internet. It is a wonderful yet dangerous digital world. Do what I do - enjoy the latest technology and use it to you advantage. Nevertheless, never underestimate the dangers that it presents. "Drive" carefully in the expressways of the cyber world.

STUDENT ESSAYS

Alexis Davila

COMPLETING HOMEWORK WITH INTEGRITY

After a long day at school, coming home to do homework can be a real drag. You sit in your seat for eight 50-minute classes, listening to the teacher go on and on about things that most of the time you do not even understand. To top it off, they give you so much homework that you barely get any time to rest at home. Let us face it though, without all the work they give us, there would not be a challenge at all. What is the fun in life without overcoming all these challenges? Being a junior at West Aurora High School is difficult. During this year, we prepare ourselves to take the ACT and take numerous classes that require that you turn in your work on time. To stay on the right path towards success, I believe that it extremely necessary that students complete their homework assignments daily and to do them with integrity.

This is true not only with school but with everything in life. For example, I can personally identify myself with this topic because I play soccer. I must practice and dedicate a great amount of time and effort in order for my team to win. As a team, winning is what we strive for. The same way that one wrong pass in a game can lead to losing a trophy, one simple mistake in your academic life can damage your future. We must understand that homework completion is to academic success what sport practices is to a championship.

As I mentioned before, soccer is what pushes me to become the best I can be. I know most of you do not know every detail about soccer; however, I know most of you do know enough to understand where I am coming from. No one hands you a trophy for showing up to the soccer game. Winning depends on all the hard work and time you have put into all the practices. In any tournament, there are many teams playing against each other and competing for the trophy; but the team that puts in the most amount of effort on the field will be the team that, at the end of the day, will go home with the victory.

It is a pain to go to practice every day of the week, starting sore from all the practices beforehand and finishing twice as sore from all the work added that day. There are two kinds of players. One who stands out for his enthusiasm, showing that he wants to win more than anything else, and the other who just goes out to the fields without any kind of drive. Completing your homework assignments on a daily basis is exactly the same thing. It will require that you consistently put a lot of effort. Many students say, "I do not have time to do my homework!" If you do not have time to complete your homework, then you must make the time! Once you have the time you need, you must use it wisely. The more wisely we spend our time, the more it will pay off in our future. I assure you that you will reach the life you have always dreamed to have.

One thing that we all need to face life challenges is integrity. Without integrity, it is very hard to achieve goals because integrity gives you the right mindset to keep your moral uprightness. History shows that we remember people not only because they were successful in life but also because they put surmounted effort into what they did and did so with integrity. They established a legacy for us to see and follow. I know that not all of us can go down in history for our personal achievements; but we can all write our own history and show that we can also achieve greatness. We can do this with help from school, family and friends. People who live and act with integrity can accomplish great things.

Undoubtedly, any decision in life can greatly influence your future. You choose whether you want to continue with your life the way it is or make changes that hopefully will lead you to success. A great example of this is Andrew Carnegie. Carnegie was a man from Scotland who immigrated into the United States with his poor parents. Not only was he poor but also disliked by many. Many people considered him unsuccessful in life. As soon as Carnegie moved to the U.S., he did not let the fact that he came from a poor background bring him down. He looked for all the opportunities his new country had to offer. After looking for what could give him vast riches, he stumbled upon an opportunity that made him the richest man in America. He saw the chance to mass produce iron, the most useful metal in the U.S. Once Carnegie perfected it, he became extremely wealthy. If Carnegie had bowed down to the thoughts and judgments of others, he would not have made the great impact he did for our society. It is important for you to understand that in spite that he was in a foreign land, he did not let others decide his future. It all comes down to the decision he made. He let his personal desire prove everyone wrong and became the most important man of his era. Many kids at school go to school and just go through the motions. Faithfully completing your homework shows that you are not one more student, just going through the motions. You will stand out because you made the personal decision to take advantage of what this country has to offer for those that get an education.

In addition to putting effort, acting with integrity and making the right decisions, we must also learn discipline. Discipline is a character trait that we learn at a young age from our parents, relatives and then school. We learn not to go over "limits" without a justifiable reason. I know as a fact that completing any task, including homework, becomes easier once you learn discipline. For example, I am very passionate about my sport, soccer; but at a young age, I did not always make the right decisions on the field. As I grew, I never had a father figure to be there for me, to support me morally or financially. I acted and played with little knowledge of the game since no one ever showed me how to play. Most importantly, I lacked the discipline needed to play well. Many times my wrong decisions on the playing field caused my team to suffer a defeat. I was just a kid without any male support! It did not take long for my coaches to understand that I did not have anyone to teach me. They not only taught me discipline, but they also taught me how to play in an intelligent manner. They taught me to give it all and not to play as if the game did to mean anything to me. It took time; but little by little, I learned discipline. The same way, doing your homework assignments every day will require that you learn and practice a lot of discipline. Discipline is necessary to learn as you mature and start to become an adult. It will help you respect "boundaries," control yourself and make good decisions in life. Discipline will help you learn more from your homework assignments because you are taking time to do them. The more your brain absorbs information the more you will act intelligently around your peers and people in general. Discipline leads to learning and learning leads to opportunities.

In conclusion, a key factor to starting down a road to success is making homework completion a daily habit and doing them with integrity. Choosing and walking the right path to become a successful person will require strength to put in the right amount of effort, do your schoolwork with integrity, make the right decisions and practice discipline.

Let us not forget that homework completion is to academic success what daily practices are to a sport championship. As an athlete, I know that what helps me be good in sports will also help me be good in school. While I am only a junior in high school, and still do not know much about how the real world works, I will continually strive to achieve greatness amongst my peers. I want to show the world that I have what it takes to achieve my dreams. If you set high goals, there is no limit to success in life.

Dr. Lourdes Ferrer

Armando J. Davila

SETTING GOALS

Throughout time, there have been individuals with great minds. Minds that helped themselves and the world be extremely successful. One of these great minds was George Washington, the first President of the United States; and others, like Mahatma Gandhi and Martin Luther King Jr., who fought for human rights with no violence. Amongst many others, Albert Einstein, the genius that developed the theory of relativity, opened doors so other minds like myself can also become great minds. However, even these great people needed to plan for success just like students who expect excellence and success in their own future should.

Greetings, my name is Armando, a junior at West Aurora High School, and let me take you on a journey in which I will speak about the importance of having short-term and long-term goals. If you anticipate a remarkable future with success on every "corner" of your life path, by any means, you cannot push back setting short and long-term goals.

Before going on, someone might be asking himself or herself, "What are those short-term and long-term goals that he is talking about?" To start off, let me tell you in general what a goal is. Goals are the final-results or outcomes of efforts. That is what both short-term and long-term goals are except for some differences. Short-term goals are the achievements that someone is trying to aim for in a short amount of time. A long-term goal is the accomplishment someone is trying to aim for a longer amount of time, or way off in terms of time. According to Dr. Lourdes, "The very first step that students must take to achieve academic and life success is to invest time and effort in planning their academic careers."

So, do you want to be a firefighter, a police officer, a teacher, a veterinarian, or even a CEO of a company? What classes you must take, or extracurricular activity should you participate, in order to prepare for the career field you want to be in? You should be thinking early on in life about these things. This also means that you should not be planning the career you want to have upon completing high school when you only have a month, a week, or even a day of high school left. On the other hand, what do you do when you do not even know where to start or what you want to be? That is okay as long as you are not at the end of you high school education.

Many schools offer courses in which students can learn and experiment different careers and see which ones they like best. Out of the school day, students can also find the "perfect" career by participating in non-school activities around their communities. These kinds of opportunities can help students identify or discover great and amazing careers, maybe the one that could be perfect for them. Just remember to invest plenty of time and a lot of effort searching and planning your academic career, if you do not want to be a mess later on.

I do not want to sound like a hypocrite because I also find myself thinking about my future and the steps that it would take. For example, I want to be a lawyer. However, what kind of lawyer do I want to be? There are too many kinds of lawyers. Honestly, I do not know! Nevertheless, what I do know is that I definitely want and need to attend college to earn a degree in law. The second step in reaching a successful life is what Dr. Lourdes says, "Students need to set short and long-term goals."

To start, it is very important that students set short-term goals once they decide the career path they are planning to take. As I said before, short-term goals are achievements that somebody can reach in a very short amount of time. Some examples of these short-term goals are completing the courses they need to graduate high school, earning specific good grades in those courses to reach or maintain a high GPA, or earning the ACT score they need for the college they want to get in. These goals are great for a senior in high school student. Depending in the grade you are in, you can have different short-term goals. Short-term goals are not limited to students who are in high school. Students in middle school (or junior high) can also have short- term goals based on the career they wish to pursue. Even students of grade school can have these goals as well. The short-term goals do not have to be a semester away; they can also be for next week or next day, like passing and getting an A in that math test.

Setting long-term goals is also very important. As I said before, a long-term goal is an achievement that a person can reach in a longer amount of time. A long-term goal is not a project that your science teacher asked you to complete in two or three weeks. You cannot reach a long-term goal immediately, even if you wanted to, because they require time to accomplish many smaller ones. In other words, a long-term goal is the sum or result of many smaller goals accomplished through time. An example of a long-term goal for high school students could be the number of college credits they will need to take per semester (or year) to earn a certificate, technical degree, or a 4-year college degree. Long-term goals are not just for high school students; they are also for junior high and even grade school students. What you should keep in mind is that time passes by fast. What you saw as long-term goal when you were younger is a short-term goal now. As a long-term goal for myself, I must plan and decide how many credits I need to take per semester (and year) to become a lawyer. According to Dr. Lourdes, the third stride we must take to be triumphant in life is deciding which steps we must take in order to reach those short and long-term goals.

After deciding which career path you are going to take and setting your short-term as well as long-term goals, it is time to figure out the steps you as a student must take to get where you want to be. Goals are futuristic but steps are now. Goals are ideas but steps are actions. For example, assuming that you have good grades, you must do whatever it takes today to maintain them that way and if you can, make them better. Right now, if the opportunity comes, participate in activities that can help you reach those goals that you have set for yourself. If you are a senior, do not wait; find out which colleges offer the degree you want to pursue. Wait! What about if you need to get a part-time job to start saving for that first year in college? Do you need money for college? How much time are you spending right now to get the free-money that you need? I want you to think about these types questions. The bottom line is, "What steps are you taking now to reach your short and long-term goals? Action steps, I my opinion, is the third piece of your life success puzzle. To be honest, the action steps that I must take right now, in order to become a lawyer is finding out scholarships that can help me finance my college education. College is too expensive! I will never become a lawyer (long-term goal) if I do not take the necessary action steps to get a law degree.

As Dr. Lourdes says, whoever does not plan is already planning to fail. The lack of planning only leads to waste of time, energy and money! Students who do not plan or set goals do not know where they are going; they have no direction. Their lack of direction does not allow them to take action steps to build the bridge from where they are to where they need to be. In my mind, like in the martial arts movies, they are walking on poles that come up from the surface instead of walking on plain floor.

Dr. Lourdes Ferrer

Christian Ramirez

BELIEVING IN YOURSELF

In the next few pages, I will help you find your potential to learn, but first let me introduce myself. My name is Christian Ramirez, and I am from Aurora, Illinois. I currently attend West Aurora, a high school with a very diverse student population. Throughout my time here at West Aurora, I have witnessed students struggling in school or not understanding the content material that the teachers are trying to teach them. In my physics class, for example, I see students who do not understand what the teacher is teaching, have problems doing their homework but are willing to ask questions to understand and improve in class. My case was different. I would simply give up when I struggled in that class and did not understand the material that was going to be tested on the test. Why? I did not believe I had the ability to understand any of the content taught in class.

Before and during the test, I knew I was going to fail. I did not know how I was going to show my mom a bad grade; however, I knew I had to! One day, my mom talked to me about what was going on with me in school. I explained to her that I did not understand anything that the teacher was teaching. I was struggling a lot! Later, she told me, "You will be able to be a better student if you become your best advocate." I have realized how much being my best advocate and believing in my potential has made me a better student, knowing that I am capable of accomplishing anything that I put my mind into doing.

I am convinced that students who believe in their potential to learn are more likely to commit, pursue a quality education, overcome academic and life challenges and even protect themselves from people who believe that Hispanics do not have what it takes to do well in school. Besides that, the students who receive plenty of help are those who believe in themselves. It makes sense. People are not going to invest their time and money in students who do not believe in their ability to succeed.

To begin with, students who believe in their potential to learn are more likely to commit and put forth the required effort to excel in school, than those who do not think they have what it takes to do well. Have you ever studied hard for a test, while others do not because they think the test was going to be easy, and then you end up receiving a better grade? I happens all the time! No matter how smart you are, you have to put forth effort to excel. I have some Spanish-speaking friends that are currently taking a regular Spanish class, but are not receiving an "A". On the other hand, I see non-Spanish speaking people receiving an "A" in that same class. The non-Spanish speaking students are putting more effort to learn the language than those whose native language is Spanish.

As I mentioned earlier, in the past I used to struggle a lot and just give up. I had no hope in myself. I always blame it on the teachers saying that they never taught the content or did not explain it clearly enough. This mentality lead me nowhere, but to a failing grade. One day my mom sat down and with a voice of disappointment said to me, "I don't want you to end up like your dad or me, working in jobs that are difficult, having to wake up early in the morning to work at a warehouse." She said to me, "It is up to you to make that final decision. If you believe you can do something good with your life, then you must know that it will require effort." Ever since, I have believed that I am capable of doing anything I commit myself to doing. My English class, for example, the class that I always disliked and never looked forward to going, is the class that I am putting the greatest effort. I want to become a better writer! I believe that I am getting better and will continue to improve. It is my belief that everyone can become more intelligent by putting the necessary effective effort.

Students who believe in themselves are empowered to overcome academic and life challenges. At some point in our life, all of us faced and overcame a school-related or life challenge. For example, in my chemistry class last year, I had a friend who believed he was going to score above 30 on the ACT. People said, "There is no way he can score that high." He believed that he was going to get the score he wanted through test preparation and help from teachers. Some students mocked him the morning before the test. The day of the ACT came. My friend came to school totally focused and determined to score good on the test. When the test was over people asked him if he felt that he scored in the 30- zone. He simply responded with a yes. Two weeks later, when the results came, he could not been any happier. He scored a 32 on the ACT! He strongly believed in himself and that he was able to score high. He was able to overcome a challenge given by his classmates and left them in shock. Up to this day, I look at him as an example of how he was able to accomplish what he really wanted the most in spite of his fellow classmates' opposition.

Sometimes, people think they can overcome challenges on their own, but this is false. Yes, you can believe you can overcome it, but it will be a lot easier with the help of other people. As you can see, my friend was able to score a 32 and overcome people's lack of belief with the help ACT tutors and teachers. He did not do it on his own; but through their help, he was able to overcome his greatest battle.

To tell you the truth, I still struggle in school. People make fun of me because they think I understand everything in class right away; but I really do not. I often seek help from my teachers and always try to complete my homework assignments with integrity. Doing homework with integrity helps students understand the material covered in class a lot better. Some students do not think I have the potential to do better and there are others who simply do not want me to have the highest grade in class. I overcome these academic challenges because I believe in myself.

Students with a strong and steady belief in their ability to learn can protect themselves from teachers', students' and even parents' low academic expectations. I can personally relate to this one because I am always looking for academic challenges. Teachers, for example, are likely to recommend us to take the classes that we can pass easily or the ones that are required for graduation. Some teachers do not even let students enroll in challenging classes because they do not think students have what it takes to be successful. I have friends that want to take more AP classes, including myself; but teachers think they would not be successful in them. I think that teachers should just recommend students to take them because it is up to the students how well they will do in those classes. These teachers have low academic expectations; that is why they only recommend the classes that are easy to pass. Dr. Lourdes Ferrer believes that a strong and steady belief in yourself is like a shield. It can protect you from others' low academic expectations. I know that challenging myself by taking demanding classes will benefit me in the end. Getting good grades, only in easy classes, will make colleges think that I am a person who wants things easy and not someone who is willing to work hard throughout his high school career. Believe in yourself and use it as a shield to protect yourself from the odds, and always strive for the hardest courses even if your teachers do not believe you can. Recently, we have been choosing our classes for the upcoming school year and I asked my teacher to recommend me for two AP science classes. At first, he thought about it and explained to me how hard that was going to be. He only wanted to put me in one. Later, I explained to him that I knew what I was getting myself into and that I was sure I could handle it. He accepted to recommend me for both and said, "You have so much belief in yourself!" If you believe, you are protecting yourself from your teachers' low expectations.

Students who believe in themselves can also reject the idea that, "Hispanics do not have what it takes to achieve the same level (or more) of academic success of other ethnic groups." For example, in my school, there are many Hispanic students but very few of them are taking AP and/or honor classes. AP and Honors classes are filled with Asian and White students. As a Hispanic, I believe that getting an education is a blessing; but many people do not realize that. They think that Hispanics will only work in low-paying jobs that do not require a college education. If that is the case, why should they bother to take classes that prepare them college? My parents and many of my friends' parents did not come to the United States to take people's jobs away, but to pursue a better life for their families. As my mom tells me quite often, "Look at what I do. I have to get up early every morning to a job I do not like; but I do it because I have to take care of you and your sister. I work hard and I will always support you in whatever you do, but please do not let me see you working at a low-paying job in the future." I have "friends" who constantly make jokes about how I will be mowing their grass and doing their landscaping work. I want these stereotypes to disappear! In the future, Hispanics might become a majority. It is our responsibility to set an example for the young ones so they can believe that we can achieve at the same level, or better than any other ethnic group.

People in general perceive students who strongly believe in themselves as high achievers. Moreover, the people who are willing and able to invest their resources will only do it with students who they believe are high achievers. I always hear my teachers saying that they will only write a letter of recommendation for students who work hard and put forth the necessary effort to do well in their classes. For example, a teacher who is willing to write you a letter of recommendation is helping you get into the college you want to attend.

A great friend of mine, who will attend college next year, told me that his teacher spoke highly about him in several colleges. Why would a teacher do that? Because she perceived him as a high achiever, she was willing to help him be accepted to any of those colleges. I know that many teachers will do their best to help students succeed; nevertheless, they are not going to waste their time and energy on students who do not try or are not willing to participate in their classes. For example, last year many of my classmates did not work hard in our geometry class because they thought that the teacher was cranky and taught in a "boring" way. Up to this day, I am glad I had him as my geometry teacher. He was always willing to help me whenever I did not understand something and even recommended me to move up to a higher math class. He knew I could do it because I believed in myself and put forth the necessary effort.

Being able to express myself through this leadership academy was truly another great blessing. I learned a lot! Quite often in my life, I have experienced many of things discussed through this academy. I recommend you to read every single competency presented in this book because it will help you believe in yourself and gain the confidence you need to overcome challenges. I want you to do everything you want to do and always think you are the best at it. Do not let negative stereotypes about Hispanics affect you. Recognize that you are capable of doing anything that you want to do, including pursuing a high-paying job. Never forget and always appreciate the great support that your parents are giving you and the amount of work they are still doing to help you have a better life. They did the impossible for you!

Christopher Rodriguez

MANAGING YOUR FINANCES

Money is only one word with two syllables; but it is what drives us as a society and makes the world go round. Some even say it talks, and you could claim that it walks and runs considering how long it remains within your account. Money is an item that can be shrouded in virtue as well as a fault. It opens doors wide open, or closes them shut completely. College is no exception to this. Thousands of students decide to go further during their high school careers. They are willing to spend more sleepless nights and longer mornings in order to achieve something greater in their education, but they simply cannot. Why? They do not have a strong financial base. This cannot continue happening! Students with great potential cannot become casualties even before going through the doors of a University.

We must be aware of our surroundings and aware of the time passing us by. As a senior at West Aurora High School, I must confess that I did not do a good job. As it stands, my financial base or resources are not where I would like them to be in order for me to attend DePaul University this upcoming September; nevertheless, I have learned from my mistakes, and I am looking for opportunities that will help me achieve my goal of attending. It is a lot of work, but it will all be worth it in the end. You cannot look at a price tag and tell yourself that it is over, and that you have no chance at meeting the costs, because there are greater costs in life. You cannot be arrogant, or stubborn, and refuse to attend a community college simply because of the things you have heard. You have to pick yourself up and be open, because this is not about your mom, your Dad or your best friend since grade school. This, going to college, is about you. Having a weak financial base is not a sign for you to quit! It is the complete opposite, it is an opportunity for you to prove to yourself that this is something that you truly want and are willing to work for. That it is an experience you will cherish, and take great care of.

Most of you are probably considering taking out a loan. You probably reassured yourself when you began reading this that most of this information would not apply to you due to the availability of loans, but I must advise you not to do what you intend. There are currently more that 30 million Americans that have an outstanding student debt. Do not become part of 30+ million. There are other options, which are harder, depending on your own strong points.

The first option is simply to get a job (and I mean early on in your high school career), whether it be something simplistic or complex, just as long as it gives you some sort of income. One of my greatest regrets as a high school student was not getting involved in the work force sooner, not opening my own account and saving for the day I needed it the most as a college student. One thing you would be wise to avoid is being over- worked, for you must always keep your health in check as my fellow writer Evelyn Gachuz will later explain. Another thing to keep in mind always is why you got the job. The last thing you would want to do is work, and merely satisfy "wants of the now" such as the newest iPhone or Jordan brand shoes. In all honesty, do you really need those things, or is it just something you want just to have it? I recently bought myself a phone that cost me around 300 dollars. The sad part of it all was that I had a phone that was in perfect condition; so, it was not a true necessity! I could have saved up that money for my education. That is not the only bad financial decision I have made, that is only the most recent.

The second option I suggest is getting involved in your community. "Community work doesn't bring economic compensation Chris?" "What are you talking about?" This might be the thoughts that are currently crossing your mind, but with all due respect, I must inform you that you are wrong, and right, and wrong. In the past few years, I have become involved in my community in various ways; one of them is by being part of this Academy. I am also part of an organization known as LULAC, or the League of United Latin American Citizens, which is grounded on community work. Due to my being involved with such groups, I began to make a name for myself. I was recognized by my school and by my city. So this, my fellow reader is where you are wrong, and right and wrong, because although community work does not provide immediate financial compensation, it will help in the end. By making a name for yourself, you make yourself someone that is worth investing in as an individual. You place yourself in a position of interest for various organizations and groups with money to invest.

The third option is to apply for scholarships! Apply! Apply! There are thousands of scholarships out there! Each with its own set of requirements, none of them too difficult to meet. Most scholarships will require you to write something, whether it be an essay or just a quick paragraph. The scholarships that I applied for all required that I write something about myself, my accomplishments, as well as my future endeavors, which should not be hard for anyone. However, you must act. Others just require that you fill out a questionnaire. Even some scholarships are awarded for merely having a distinct physical feature, as orange eyes and wings (ha-ha); but seriously, there are scholarships that you can find if you look hard enough and act quickly enough to catch them. The school of your choice might also have scholarships of its own offered to applicants and accepted students.

The fourth and last option, which for some strange reason is frowned upon by many students, is attending a community college for the first two years of their college education. This option saves students a great amount of money considering that tuition at a community college is not that high. It also helps you get your general education classes, like math, science, and English out of the way, which means that when it comes time for you to transfer out, you will only take classes that will focus on your field of study. Community college has always been an option that I have kept in mind throughout my high school career, just in case that I am not able to attend the college of my choosing.

All of these options are out there, within my state, and yours. You cannot let a lack of money limit you as a person with so much potential. You have to have self-control and that same drive you show within the classroom, or on and off the field. There are also moments when you must swallow your pride, and understand that you cannot go to the college of your dreams (just yet). The bottom line is that you can feel like a college casualty even before you start college, when you know you have no options due to the lack of money. Nevertheless, not having the money you need or want, and getting yourself into a lot of debts, will definitely make you a college casualty after you are through with college, when the debt starts coming in from all of the loans. So be proactive, be strong, and go out to get what you have worked for your whole life.

Dr. Lourdes Ferrer

David Ballines

NURTURING YOUR INTELLIGENCE

Many high school students believe that they just do not have the ability to learn. A high percentage of students has a philosophy stuck in their head that some people are just born intelligent and have the ability to learn and that the others can never be intelligent or are not able to learn too well. That kind of mindset can continue throughout their college careers. Dr. Lourdes Ferrer believes that this philosophy is incorrect. She believes that all students, not some, have the ability to become intelligent and learn more than they believe they can.

As a junior at West Aurora High School, I have seen many students not participate in activities because they think they do not have the natural talent to succeed. I am talented in mathematics because I have nurtured it enough to participate in math competitions. For a fact, I know that I do not have any talent in singing. Just hear me sing and you will have your ear drums ruptured! I know that some people are more talented in certain areas than others; but we all have the ability to learn if we nurture it, feed it and make it grow. Students who do not believe in their potential to learn give up when they face challenges. They stop doing homework, studying for tests, and paying attention to the teacher in class during class. I strongly believe that students who do not nurture their ability to learn will never reach their full potential and goals in life.

There are many different ways for someone to nurture their natural ability to learn. These include committing to learning, working hard to reach their learning goals, focusing on learning, getting feedback from teachers or peers, motivating themselves to learn, and strategizing on how to reach learning goals. If students use these techniques to nurture their ability to learn, they will be successful in learning even if they are not sure they have what it takes.

Some students are not committed to learn, and no matter how much people try to make them study and learn, they do not do it. From personal experience, I know that people do not like to get involved in things that require some sort of effort. For example, a member of my wrestling varsity team quit just because he lost all of his motivation. He did not want to wrestle anymore and just quit even though he was an extremely good wrestler. Evidently, he was not committed. Just like sports, learning is also an arduous task, which takes commitment and motivation to learn and become more intelligent. You need to have the desire to study and nurture your ability to learn in order to stay in school. Nurturing your capacity to learn by being committed, and motivated to learn is the first step towards becoming more intelligent and reaching your career goals.

Working hard and "just working" are two very different things and have different effects on the way someone can learn. While both "working hard" and "just working" can advance your learning process, there is a big difference between the two. When you work hard, you put everything you have into learning and accomplish much more than, if you are just doing the minimal work required to pass the class. Students who work hard to learn something is just like athletes who "play hard" to beat the opposing team. The athlete who works the hardest is likely to come out on top; reinforcing the idea that the harder people work, the more they can advance in the career they pursue. Hard work is hard for a reason! Although putting your all into learning is not easy, in the end the payoff is much greater and more pleasing than just coasting by and not working as hard. Nurturing your natural ability to learn by working hard as you can, will definitely increase your ability to learn and reach your academic and career goals.

You might believe you have done everything correctly so far. You are doing your schoolwork, you have a decent plan for the future and you have made the right decisions. Nevertheless, without any feedback from teachers, peers, or qualified adults, you cannot really know if you are in the right path. That is why I believe that all students should take advantage of their teachers' desire to help them. Most teachers are more than willing to give their students feedback regarding their work in class to help them become more intelligent, better students and stay on the right track. Teachers' feedback regarding your schoolwork will help you see your errors and understand the mistakes you made so you do not make them again. Most people agree that the best way to learn is from your mistakes. Getting feedback on schoolwork is extremely beneficial for you to become more intelligent. Not getting feedback is like driving in the dark without any headlights. You do not know where you are going, or even if you are going in the right direction. The lack of feedback can kill your academic future in an instant.

Staying focused is as important as committing, working hard and getting continuous feedback. During the school year, students should stay focused on their studies and not worry about anything else. Staying focused helps students learn more and better and stay on track with their schoolwork. Staying focused requires having your priorities right. For example, can you stay focus on your schoolwork if you go out with your friends every night? Going out every night surely diminishes students' ability to learn. Very soon, they will only care about the friends and their learning will suffer. If the time spent going out with friends is spent studying, then students can nurture their ability to learn, become more intelligent and succeed in any career of their choice.

Even if you do everything that I mentioned in this paper, your efforts can be in vain or wasted if you do not strategize properly. You must have strategies in place to succeed in school and in life. You have to know what you need to do (and not do) to make things work out for you. In a football game, you can have the best team; but if the team does not know any of the plays and has not strategized before the game, they will surely fail. Students who plan their future as soon as possible can see the hurdles they will be face. For example, what financial issues will I face? Which transportation will I use to go to school? With things like this in mind, students are better able to strategize. They will be empowered to face challenges a lot easier and better. Students who strategize can deal with problems as soon as possible, which means they can spend more time worrying about their academic work instead of a dealing with financial or transportation issues.

Having a strategy also helps students take advantage of all of the time they have available so they can focus or concentrate on their schoolwork. The best or easier way to strategize is when you already have short and long-term goals. Your goals will determine the strategies that you need to stay on the path of becoming more intelligent and achieving academic and life success.

Nature has given every single individual in this planet an amazing gift, not just a select few. The gift nature gave us is the ability to learn, but the gift can just go to waste if individuals like you and me do not nurture it. Dr. Lourdes Ferrer compares the gift to learn to an apple seed. Enough nurturing and care will help the apple seed become a great tree. However, that same seed will rot and go to waste if it does not receive the proper care. It is very important for you to nurture your ability to learn, even if you do not totally believe in yourself. If you set your mind to it and follow the vigorous path of becoming more intelligent and learning, you can become a great apple tree and grow big with knowledge and intelligence.

Dr. Lourdes Ferrer

Evelyn Ganchuz

MEETING YOUR BASIC NEEDS

My name is Evelyn Gachuz. I was born in Aurora Illinois and I am currently a student at West Aurora High School. In my four years of high school, I have discovered the importance of maintaining physical, social, and emotional health. I have learned a few things about it from experience, which is why I chose to share my ideas regarding this strategy with you.

In order to grow and succeed as a person, we need to have a strong and sturdy foundation, one that we can build on. The problem is that we, as students living in stressful environments with many worries and responsibilities, tend to put ourselves last when it should be our priority. Abraham Maslow once said, "What a man can be, he must be. This need we call self-actualization." This means that every person should strive to reach their potential in life and be the best they can be. Maslow, the American psychologist who created the hierarchy of needs, believed that every person needed to fulfill their basic needs in order to become self-actualized. Physical, social and emotional health, are some of the basic needs every human being has.

We cannot take steps toward reaching our goals without experiencing emotional well-being. Worries, concerns, and negative thinking can cloud our minds and distract us from our goals. Adolescence is an emotional stage in our lives and all these emotions can be very distracting. Students who worry a lot have a hard time concentrating, making it harder to do well in school, pay attention in class, and get a quality education. I believe that taking time to relax after a long day at school is a way for students to release some stress.

It is very important that students also have a positive self-image. A positive self-image provides students the confidence they need to complete their school assignments and other responsibilities in life. A friend of mine found this very difficult to do. She had an older sister that was always picking on her. She would always tell my friend that she was not good enough to the point that my friend began to believe it. For some time my friend felt worthless and had a very low self-esteem. Her grades began to slip and she did not feel or had the energy to do the things she always enjoyed doing. I have learned in life that there will always be people like my friend's sister who enjoy putting others down; nevertheless, we should not let it bother us. Knowing who we are and having a strong self-worth will help us counteract the negative impact of people like that. My friend soon learned how not to let her sister's comments bother her anymore. She realized she was beautiful! No one cannot tell her otherwise. We all struggle to keep a positive self-image at times; we just need to learn ways to remind ourselves of our strengths. Nicholas Barrios will surely address this topic with details. I must also say that comfort and safety can bring confidence to a person. We need to feel safe in order to take the necessary steps toward reaching our goals. Positive thinking is also a practice that can help us experience emotional well-being.

The lack of health and physical well-being is another barrier that could stand in the way of reaching our potential and goals in life. For example, as students we have busy lives filled with school responsibilities and activities. Besides that, we have part-time jobs, practice sports, run chores and have friend and families who demand our attention. Trust me. Getting eight hours of sleep seems impossible! The lack of sleep does not allow students to concentrate the next day in class. Sleep allows our brains to store memories so we can remember the information we learned during the day in school. Sleep and rest are essential for awareness and focus throughout the day. The bottom line here is that students cannot be at their best if they are exhausted and tired. That is why it is so important to make sleep a priority.

Another thing that we sometimes neglect to do is eat healthy. For the sake of time, we often rush and buy fast food or we skip a meal altogether. Doing this does not allow us to get all the energy we need, which in the end will have a negative impact in our lives. My older cousin started college two years ago. It was the first time he lived on his own. In high school, he was into wrestling and eating healthy; but once he started college, he did not have time to cook proper meals and instead bought fast food. Not only he felt always tired but he also gained weight. College students joke about the "freshman fifteen," which means that freshman students will gain fifteen pounds during their first year in college. It is funny but it actually happens very often. Therefore, as student we need to set time aside to make proper meals. We must learn recipes of quick and healthy meals to stay healthy and be at our best. Sleep, exercise, and a healthy diet are all important to take care of our bodies.

Finally yet importantly, we must also secure social health. As human beings, one of our most important needs is to have healthy relationships with our family members and friends who can bring us feelings of comfort and safety. They are the ones we can count on to help us during hard times, when we need advice from people who really care about us. Everyone needs a break from school and work occasionally and it is okay to have fun and take the stress off everything. I knew a very smart girl who really works hard in school and sports. The problem was that, while focusing solely in school activities, she did not spend as much time with her friends and family as she used to. She was stressed-out most of the time because she never had time to relax! I noticed that she was not as happy as she used to be and got sick very often. All the work she was doing was too much for her. Her family and friends really missed her. It is a good thing to care about grades, but not at the expense of everything else in life. I believe there should be a balance between the time we spend in school-related activities and the time we spend with family and friends. Things have changed now. She finally is finding time during her busy week to spend time with her family and friends. She is much more relaxed. The relationships we maintain with family and friends will follow us throughout our lives. They play an important role in our happiness making them essential to our total well-being.

To begin the journey toward becoming who we want to be in life and reaching our potential, we must first meet our human basic needs. We cannot arrive at our destinations without maintaining our physical, emotional, and social health. Meeting our basic needs will empower us to strive for success, knowing that we have built a foundation strong enough to firmly stand and not fall down. Our mind and body are parts of who we are and will be with us for the rest of our lives. That is why taking care of them should be our priority.

Hesiquio Ballines

SEEKING ACADEMIC PROFICIENCY

Many times during a week at school I hear, "When are we ever going to use this?" or "Why are we even learning this?" Though I hear this mostly during my math class, I also hear it during my English class, especially when we are writing and reading. The best and must simple answer is, "You will definitely never need this in a minimum wage job. Is that what you want?" What teenagers my age do not understand is that reading, writing, mathematics, and being able to use technology in a productive way are very important and arguably the most needed academic subjects for college success. I chose this topic because I got annoyed after hearing the same thing, over and over again. These four academic proficiencies are like the four wheels of a car. The same way that it is very difficult to drive a car with a flat tire, it is very difficult to achieve academic success when you are "low" in any of these academic areas.

However, this still does not answer the question, "When are we ever going to use this?" Many careers require these proficiencies, including engineers, chemist, journalist, mechanic, computer programming, or even a cashier. After naming these four proficiencies, I must explain how to develop them. "Well, "Studying will do the job," some people might say; but it is not that simple. Studying does help students improve in any of these areas; but to some it will require a lot more effort.

To begin with, reading gives you independent access to all the information you need to get to where you need to be. This may seem obvious; but there is more to it than simply understanding the English language and having the ability to read. You must not only be able to read somewhat quickly, but also have the ability to comprehend what you are reading. This is something I struggle with personally. Many times while reading, I start thinking about what I am going to do later in the day. After reading what I was supposed to read I was not able to summarize or explain what I just read. In order to fix this problem, I had to have someone to "quiz" me; that is, to ask me to explain in my own words what the passage was about. You can also break the reading in smaller chunks and then increase the amount of text you read or move to something longer. This strategy will insure that you remain focused on what you are reading and able to keep a lot of information in your head.

Another problem other people face is their reading speed. Personally, I did not suffer or struggled with my speed. However, I know the reason why. In order to fix this problem, you can find reading material about things that you are interested in. Something you must realize is that it does not have to be a book. For example, I love to read about the latest technology and video games. Therefore, I read tons of articles about it to the point that it has increased my reading speed. If video games are not "your thing," then there are many other things to read about, like skateboarding, weird plants and animals, the latest fashion trends or gossip about celebrities like Justin Bieber. These kinds of tactics can help you improve your reading ability. It will help you in college because it will greatly shorten the time spent reading a textbook and gathering information. Reading faster will give you extra free time to cram more information into your brain or to keep your sanity by doing something that entertains you.

The second of the four "wheels" is writing proficiency. Students, who are competent writers, can effectively communicate their thoughts and feeling, which is obvious. You will agree with me that it takes a lot more effort than just knowing "how to write" or being familiar with the English language. A problem that many people face in writing, something that I personally struggle with, is getting my thoughts together and putting them in writing. Thinking or saying something is very different from writing. A solution for this is to look up a topic on the internet, it could be something or something controversial, and begin writing a paragraph or two about it. See how much time did it take you to write your thoughts about that topic in a single paragraph. If you continue to repeat this process repeatedly, you will soon get better and faster in putting your ideas together. Something people also struggle with is grammar. I hope that you can see by my writing that I do not have a problem with this. Something that really helped me with this was to write and always look back to see the mistakes I made. After doing this several times, you will learn to catch most of your mistakes while you are writing rather than after you are done. This is very important. Your essay papers will now look nicer and you might even be able to save a little time on spell checking or questioning if a comma is in the right spot.

Math proficiency, the third of the "wheels" also builds your capacity to solve or deal with all kinds of academic and life challenges. Mathematics is probably the most hated class in school. This is the subject that my fellow classmates complaint the most. Maybe you will not use many of the formulas learned in an Algebra class. Maybe you do not want to be an engineer, architect, or anything that involves high technology. Nevertheless, for all of you actors and artists, math can be very helpful; but not for the reason you may think. Math is a very difficult subject to master; it is all about solving problems. Mastering mathematics makes solving problems in in the real world a lot easier. I usually do not struggle with math; however, I have encountered "a couple" of challenging ones that I did not know how to solve. When I did not have the knowledge or skills to solve the problem, I got help. The assistance you might need does not necessarily have to come from your math teacher. When I am not able to solve a math problem, I ask a friend to help me analyze it. This has actually helped me many times although it might look like "cheating."

Finally yet importantly, technology, the fourth of the "wheels" is the platform that will allow you to maximize your chances to compete and reach your academic and career goals. This one is the most fun to talk about because it is something we teenagers use every single day of our lives; however, we tend to use it for the wrong purposes. For example, most people spend their precious time taking "selfies" in the bathroom and posting them on Facebook. They seem to ignore the fact that the internet offers many online resources that could help them finish their homework. I am not saying that posting on Facebook or playing games online is a bad thing. What I am saying is that students need to be aware that there are many sources available to help them do better in school. For example, someone who does not know how to solve a math problem can look for a video tutorial in YouTube. Microsoft Word, for example, can help you create documents in a more organized fashion. Microsoft PowerPoint can also help you make impressive presentations for any class.

Finally, after going through the specifics of how you can improve in each of these four proficiencies, I must say that there are other "general methods" for improving. People who want to improve in anything must commit, focus, work hard, and seek feedback. Commitment is big! How can people improve in anything they are not committed to learn? For example, how will you become the best skateboarder if you are not willing to commit to learning any tricks? Hard work is also a very important thing. Improving in something you are not good at will require hard work. How can you improve in sport without putting hard work during practice? Seeking and receiving feedback in the area that you want to improve is also very important. How will you know how you are doing if you do not get feedback from others? Feedback does not always have to be from other people. Standardized test scores, like the ACT, are useful because they show your intellectual ability, even more than your G.P.A. Why? Because your grade point average can sometimes include extra credit or points for class participation. It is like getting the "Hardest Worker Award." It is okay; I received one of those before. Even though you worked the hardest, it does not always reflect how well you performed.

In conclusion, everyone can improve these four academic proficiencies using the methods or tactics I presented in this essay. Just make sure that you keep all of these skills sharp because you will need them in college and the rest of your life. So, stay motivated and show the world that you have what it takes to be successful. Disprove all those people who tell you that you are dumb and make your parents proud. I assure you that I will be doing the same thing.

Irving Espinoza

REACHING DIGITAL LITERACY

I want to start this essay stating that, I believe that many of my same-age peers are not using technology to their benefit. I remember once, when I was a bit younger, that I stayed home twitting for hours. I really thought I had nothing to do. Nevertheless, the next day at school, I remembered that I had homework. I totally forgot about it! Many students today are doing the same thing, constantly using technology the wrong way. What a waste of time! I used three hours on my phone time just twitting. I could had just put my phone down and do my homework. Then I would not have to worry about it the next day. Most people have computers, different computer software, Smart phones, T.V., and internet access, and yet they are not using it to benefit themselves academically. Instead of using it for dumb and irrelevant purposes, we should use all these kinds of new technologies for more important reasons, such as meeting our academic needs.

When I was younger, my first source for information were my parents. However, there is a point in life when they cannot help you anymore. In my case, when I grew older and reached a certain grade level, my parents could not help me anymore with any of my academic subjects. They did not have the academic background or knowledge to answer many of my questions or help me with my homework assignments. For example, no matter how much they wanted to, they could not help me with my math assignments. I had to find a different source of information. A computer connected to the internet became that source! By clicking, I was able to get all the help I needed. The internet is a great and reliable source of information, especially for students like me, whose parents do not have the academic background to help them with school-related things.

That is what I love the most about my generation. You do not need to be wealthy to get the information or academic assistance that you need. Years ago, you had to have the money to pay someone to help you learn or better understand something that your teacher covered in class.

There are tons of websites now that you can visit and get the help you need; and you can do that at any time and in any place. Money, time or place is no longer an issue! Do you need help with your science class or a science project? Go online, "surf the net," and get the help you need. For example, YouTube has thousands of videos that can teach you anything you want to learn. There are thousands of tutorial programs for all kinds of academic subjects. Let us imagine that your math teacher introduced a new subject, for example, inequalities. In spite that he spent the entire period teaching students how to solve inequities, you left the class very confused. Guess what? All you have to do is go online and visit, for example, the Khan Academy website. This website is loaded with hundreds (if not thousands) of videos in which the math professor Khan teaches you, step-by-step, how to solve any math problem. In this case, you just need to type, "solving inequalities," and right there, at that same moment, you will get videos that systematically will teach you how to do it. If you do not understand something, just press the rewind key and you will see and hear the same thing as many times as you want. You cannot do that with a teacher. Right? Teachers do not have rewind buttons.

According to Dr. Lourdes Ferrer, technology is the great equalizer. Computers connected to the Internet, for example, have given everyone the same opportunity to succeed academically. The difference between students who do well in school and those that do not, is not the money they have or who their parents are. The difference is their willingness to put in the necessary effort to learn how to use the latest technology that is available to all of us. In our generation, saying that we are too lazy or do not have enough time is no longer an excuse. Technology has made things easier for all of us.

Computers programs such as Microsoft PowerPoint or Microsoft Word can help all students excel in school. You can get good grades and improve your GPA by creating excellent and impressive documents. With Power Point, you can design and facilitate informative and lively presentations. Power Point has functions or tools that allow you to present your ideas in a creative and interesting way. You can insert visuals, sounds and even videos, which gets people engaged. The Microsoft Word program can help you write papers easier and faster, especially if you know how to type. For example, writing an essay paper using Word is easier and faster than doing it the "old way," with pen and paper. You can bold, underline, change the color of words or sentences, which will help you catch the reader's attention, while helping you communicate your ideas better. More than anything else, you can turn in papers free of spelling errors. You can even find out the number of words you used, especially when you need to write something using a certain number of words. What can be better than that? You can impress people when you use these programs.

Another way that the internet can help students reach their academic goals is that they can go online and look for colleges. They can find the best college for the specific career that they are planning to pursue. For example, if you are interested in colleges that specialize in medicine, you just need to go online. Like some people say, "just google it!" In less than a second it will show you which schools are the best. Whatever you do not know and want to know, the internet will always be there for you. Even if you do not know how to cook something, you can go online to learn how to do it. The internet can also help you find the financial aid you need to attend that college that you found online. You can seek hundreds of scholarship programs at the same time. This can greatly increase your chances of gaining the financial aid you need to pursue the career of your dreams. Sadly, many students do not take advantage of this. They end up applying for student loans and charging things to credit cards; and if they ever graduate, they will do so with huge amount of debts. Graduating with big debts is a terrible thing! All your salary will go to paying loans or credit card debts. As you can see, if you know how to go online and search for things, you can choose the college that is best for you and get the money you need to pay for it. All you need is a computer, internet access and the skills to search online.

One of the things that I like the most about technology is that it has given all of us the opportunity to communicate easier and faster. There so many different social media websites, including Twitter, Facebook, Instagram and Skype. These media websites allow people around the world to communicate and connect with each other. A message can reach a person at "the speed of light." What I mean is that any message, whether is a text, a twit, an email, etc., can get to a person in less than a second. How powerful is that! You can send a message to your teacher, a peer or any person who can help you with school, after school hours. You can turn-in a paper on time if you send it via email to your teacher as an attachment. You can invite others to join you in a study group with a twit or through Facebook. Are you working on a project? Use Skype! You can communicate with people face-to-face. You can do it through your computer and even with your phone, if they have internet access, of course. Technology has revolutionized the way we communicate with each other. It does not matter how far a person is. Through the internet, we can stay in touch and work together. Although all of this is awesome, my concern is that too many young people use these "speedy" ways of commination for non-essential things, such as posting stupid things on media sites like Facebook or Twitter. Some use Skype for wrong and dangerous things. What many students might not be aware is that whatever they post on line is public. Once you send it, you cannot get it back. For example, employers who are considering hiring people can easily access these messages. They might change their minds and not hire people after they see what is on their "Facebook Wall" or "Twitter Feed." People can also create a video of what you are doing when you Skype. That video can end up anywhere and affect your reputation forever. As you can see, these new technologies can open many doors; but can also close them forever. It all depends how we use them.

Another great way that technology has improved people's lives is that it has created an enormous amount of new and interesting jobs. Companies, more than ever before, are looking for people who are competent in the use of the latest technology. It is very hard or maybe impossible to get a decent job today that does require basic computer skills. All of them do!

In conclusion, technology will continue to grow and advance. Your ability to use the latest technology to improve academically will determine the kind of career that you will be able to pursue. On one hand, students must do whatever it takes to increase their computer knowledge and skills. On the other hand, they must avoid at all cost using it for the wrong reasons. The internet is a wonderful and yet dangerous thing. Students need to be tech-smart!

Jimena Moreno

OVERCOMING CHALLENGES

Life always throws unplanned situations in our way. I strongly believe that the best way to "take on" these situations is to recognize what they are, understand why they happen and then accept that things might not come out as planned. We must tell ourselves to move forward even if things get harder than before. Everyone on this earth faces all kinds of challenges; of course, not all challenges are the same, some are bigger than others are. I have learned that as challenges come our way, we will grow and learn new things, not only about ourselves but also about the world that we live in. However, for us to grow or achieve our dreams we must recognize, understand and have the ability to overcome whatever challenge life presents to us.

My biggest personal challenge right now is the financial problems that my family is facing. As a junior at West

Aurora High School, I know it is time to start researching colleges to find out which one is the best one for me. At least, this is what people are constantly telling me to do. After hours and days researching colleges, I finally found one that I was "head over heels" for! I fell in love with everything about St. Louis University! However, the very last thing I looked into was the amount of money I needed to attend my "dream" university. I knew college was going to be expensive. Nevertheless, no one ever told me it was going to be thousands of dollars, thousands of dollars my parents do not have. I talked to my parents and my older brother about how I found my "perfect" university; however, once I mentioned how much it was going to be, their facial expressions said it all. All my hopes and dreams came crashing down! We could not afford this college. If I were someone raised with no motivation or support from my family, I would have stopped trying completely. However, it does not work that way. If you cannot get what you wish for, do not stop there. Life does not stop to wait for you. You have to have the strength to not let it ruin you completely and to be able to move on from it. There are many scholarships, grants, and programs out there that can help me achieve my dreams. Whether it is going to my dream college or not, I am not going to let money define me. I am going to do the best I can to get where I want to be. This should apply to everyone. Do not let anyone or anything get in the way of pursuing your dreams. As you can see, I recognized what my problem was, understood why it was a problem for me and then knew I had the ability to overcome it.

I believe that Hispanic students in particular, face certain circumstances that are much different and much harder than what other students face. A personal problem that many Hispanic students confront in school is their lack of proficiency in core academic subjects, meaning they struggle to maintain decent grades in courses they are required to pass in order to graduate. Whether it is because of things going on at home with their families, things going on between peers at school, or simply because they do not understand the content material, somehow students need to find the help they need. If you cannot help yourself, find someone you can trust to help you out so your grades and Grade Point Average (GPA) do not suffer. If the strategies you are using now are not working, then it is necessary to find someone who can help you out. Whether it involves asking for help from a teacher, a tutor, or even a friend, some students simply have a problem with seeking help. Trust me! Do not think that you can carry on in this hectic world by yourself, without the help of others. As my peer Rudy Lozano says, "Don't let the problem hold you back and don't surrender to it." Other people have gone through the problems you are facing. They got through them and learned much from them; so why not let their experiences help keep you on the right track?

I also think that a challenge that many Hispanic students face is not having sufficient or no support at all from their own families. These students do not have parents who can support and monitor their academic careers because of two main reasons. The first is that the parents' level of education is lower than their children's level of education. For example, there are more opportunities for people to receive an education here in the United States than in their native countries. Not speaking English is also one of the most basic struggles Hispanic parents also face, which does not let them get involved or support their children's academic lives.

As a middle school student, there were times I would come home from school stressed out because I did not understand some of the things I had to do for homework.

My parents always wanted to help me because they knew how upset I would become. Sadly, they would show a blank stare in their eyes when I explained to them what my problem was. Neither one of them understood what I was talking about because when they were younger, they did not have the education we have here in the United States. Both of them made an effort though. They would try to explain certain things they did know about the subject to see if that would help; sometimes it did, but other times it did not. When it did not help, I would get so frustrated to the point that I did not even want to try anymore. I would talk so much crap about how horrible the teachers were because I could not do my homework. I would just refuse to do my homework just to make my parents suffer! However, my mom used to give me a look that said, "What in the world are you saying?" The teachers already had their degrees. Talking about the teachers was not going to get me anywhere. Life went on whether I did my homework or not, whether I passed a test or not. All of this at the end would only affect me; so I had to raise my head up, stop being negative and prove to everyone (even myself) that I could do it. She would then tell me to relax and to read everything all over again until I understood it. I realized she was right in every way.

Even though my parents could not help me with my homework, they supported me and motivated me to keep on trying. When many kids speak with their parents nowadays, they do not even let them talk. Stop! Let them talk because I am very sure they did not go through "hell" to get here to the United States just to watch you fail. They want to see you succeed and I am sure that you have what it takes to make them proud. Do not become a "nobody" when you have the potential to become a "somebody."

Lastly, another challenge that many Hispanic students face is their home environment. As a Hispanic myself, I know how important family is to us, not only parents and siblings, but also grandparents, uncles, aunts and cousins. For different reasons, many of our extended family members end up living with us. For example, suppose that your mom's sister lost her home. Because her husband left her, she needs a place to stay until she can save enough money to get an apartment for herself and her kids. Even though that the house is already extremely crowded because it is tiny, you know that your mom is not going to let her sister roam around homeless. That is just how we

Hispanics are. We help people in their time of need, even if we need help ourselves. Finding a quiet space to do your homework or study for a test is not easy in a full house, especially when the house is small. Just imagine! Little kids are running around the house. The television is on with shows that distract you from your work. Your uncle and aunt are fighting because one of them forgot to pay a bill that was due yesterday. Your cousin is blasting music trying to block out everyone else's noise. Your dad is in the garage fixing your brother's car that just broke down. Your grandmother is complaining about how much she misses her home while your mom is yelling at you because you forgot to clean your room. This is hectic, isn't it? How can anyone get his or her homework done in a house like this? Should you even do it? Even if you tried to concentrate in a home like this, you will never experience the silence you can enjoy in a library, a place where you can relax and your mind can focus on your schoolwork. Oh look! You found a solution to your problem! You recognized that your home is full of activities that do not let you accomplish your homework assignments. You understand that if you do not find a peaceful place to complete your assignments you will not be able to turn them in and they are due tomorrow.

You have the ability to overcome this by simply asking your parents for permission to go to the library, which I highly doubt they would say no to. Unbelievably, little things like this will make a difference in your life. You cannot let situations like this keep you from completing your homework.

In conclusion, life is like a box of chocolates. You never know what you are going to get. That is why you must prepare yourself for a "crazy" world full of unexpected challenges. Things do get rough! Big or small, keep in mind that your success in life will depend on your ability to recognize, understand and overcome every personal challenge. I know you will be able to achieve all the greatness you have always wished to achieve. Here is one thing I want you to "stick in your head." Never quit when things get rough because what does not kill you will only make you stronger.

Karina Callegos

ESTABLISHING CONNECTIONS

My name is Karina Gallegos and I am a senior at West Aurora High School. I was born in Mexico and moved to the United States almost four years ago. Since I came here, my parents and I knew that we were going to need plenty of help from others; and this because my parents knew very little about the American educational system. As a family, we strongly believe that a quality education is the key to a quality life or a better future here in the United States. At the same time, we also believe that a good education depends on students, parents, and teachers. In order to succeed academically, I strongly believe that students must make positive and productive connections with their teachers and/or professionals that can assist them when needed.

When I came to this country, I had to face many challenges. Most of those challenges had to do with my education. If it were not for teachers and counselors, my parents and I would have had a harder time understanding the school system, solving school-related problems or making decisions regarding my education.

As a student, I am always trying to show or prove to my teachers how important education is to me. I feel that making good connections with them will help me be a better student. When I feel connected with my teachers, my classes are easier. I enjoy going to class and feel comfortable asking questions. Every time I have a difficult time understanding something, I look for help until I find it. My first choice is the teachers. I instantly look for them because they are the best qualified to give me all the information that I need. They never judge or criticize me when I am having problems in class or I do not understand something. After being in high school for four year, I concluded that open communication with teachers could increase students' confidence in class.

Having a good connection with teachers can also open doors to academic and life success. Teachers are usually people with plenty of life experiences. People, who are experienced, can give students good advice. They are able to recognize when "something" is good or bad because they have already gone through those experiences. When a teacher or a professional has the opportunity to guide a student, I know by experience that they will do it to the best of their abilities.

I am aware that some students might have a hard time establishing a connection with their teachers. The best way to start, in my opinion, is to show them that you really want a good education. You have to show them that you are not in school because you do not have any other choice. My advice to you is that if you want to connect with your teachers, always try to sit at the front of the classroom. Avoid sitting at the back as if you want to be far away from them. Share with your teachers some important educational facts about yourself. It is important that teachers get to know who you are. The sooner you do that the better. Show great interest in what they are teaching. Teachers like that! Follow the teacher's instructions. That way your make their work easier. Most of all, always maintain a positive attitude towards your teachers and in class.

Some students think they can do everything by themselves. That is false! As teenagers, we will always need some kind of assistance from people who know more than you and me because we are still exploring and learning. For example, you might need help solving a math problem, finding the main idea of an article or creating a Power Point presentation. Teachers can help you! Guidance counselors can also help you decide which college to apply or which courses to take next year. These connections can help you reach your goals easier and faster. I always receive help from my teachers every time I do not understand something in class. I am also confident that if I ask them, they will write me a letter of recommendation. The school counselor will also help me apply for scholarships. Teachers and counselors are more able and willing to help students that they know personally, especially those who show that they care about their education. It is difficult to help someone you do not know. Right?

Teachers and counselors have the ability to listen and be patient, more than people of your own age and even family members. At least that has been my experience with them. Teachers and other professionals many times can see and believe in students' abilities; they see students' potential! They can give students the hope and confidence they need to better themselves. As Dr. Lourdes says, "Having a person on your side, who is there for you when you need it, is like carrying your personal GPS. He or she knows where you are and how to get you where you need to be in your academic path."

From my own experience, I have learned and accomplished many things thanks to my teachers. A strong teacher-student relationship can make a difference in how successful a student can be. Please, do not get me wrong! When I say a good teacher-student relationship, it does not mean that students should have a personal relationship outside of school. That is not necessary. That is why you have your friends and family. A good teacher-student relationship takes place in school; but it has the power to help you succeed beyond the school walls.

A student cannot have a positive connection with a teacher if the student is constantly giving the teacher a hard time in class. The student needs to put forth effort and have a positive attitude in class. I do not think this kind of connection will form naturally. It requires effort! There are some little actions that can help you build a good connection with teachers, such as attending school every day, coming to class on time, doing your homework every day (and doing it with integrity), and showing great respect towards them in class.

A good relationship produces a good environment in the classroom, for both the teacher and the student. Students who have a good relationship with their teachers will achieve at a higher level than those who do not have a positive connection. When a teacher feels a good connection with the students, the classroom environment becomes more enjoyable, teachers and students interact in a respectful manner, and teachers are more willing to offer students help.

Melissa Medellin

REACHING ASSESSMENT LITERACY

According to Dr. Maria de Lourdes, "You must accept the idea that taking tests is a big slice of your academic pie." As students, we must open our eyes to this reality. It is the truth! Standardized assessments measure how proficient students are in key subject areas like math, reading, and science. Test- taking is an important component in identifying one's academic strengths and weaknesses, which can determine the kind of lifestyle we can afford in the future. As a junior at West Aurora High School, I am currently preparing myself to take the ACT. The scores that I get in this test will decide the college that I can attend and my possibilities of enrolling in a college career that is in high demand and pays well. During one of the sessions of the *Grooming for Excellence Academy Student Leadership Academy*, directed by Dr. Lourdes, she told us that although her GPA graduating from high school was a 4.0, she "was the best among the worst," due to her placement test scores for college. She did not pass any of the test's sections, not even Spanish! I learned that a student's GPA does not always tell the whole truth about his or her level of academic proficiency. When I became aware of this, I was automatically interested in this competency, which states that students know the purpose, use, and format of every assessment they take. Reaching assessment literacy, or really understanding tests, is the key to academic success.

Standardized testing primarily focuses on the key subjects such as math, reading, and science. These three subjects are the most important because we use them every day. Understanding and having the ability to score high in these three areas can get you far in life, whether you are studying for a career in aviation or nursing, it does not matter. I think we already know that the most important tests in the state Illinois are the ISAT (Illinois Standards Achievement Test) and the PSAE (Prairie State Achievement Examination), which includes the ACT. The students take the ISAT from third to eighth grade and the PSAE in 11th grade.

It is important to know that a students' performance on these tests have tremendous impact their academic lives.

For example, the ISAT measures how much you know so that teachers can help pick your classes in high school. High scores on the ISAT can give students opportunities to enroll in honor classes during high school. That is one of the many purpose of the ISAT. The same goes for the ACT. As we said before, the scores that you get in this test will determine the college you could qualify to attend. Knowing what assessments like the ISAT and the ACT are testing will give you a good opportunity to prepare yourself to do well. Preparation is a big part of doing well in any test and achieving great academic goals.

Armando, my friend, believes that planning is also one of the big mechanisms to achieve your academic and life goals. There is no way around it. You must have a plan in mind in order to succeed! It is for this reason that the first step to doing well in any assessment is to plan how to prepare for it. You and I need to review all the material that the test will cover. I have heard teachers saying that students cannot really prepare for tests such as the ISAT. I do not agree with them. If you know the content material tested on any test, then you are able to review it and be better prepared to do well. In my opinion, the assessment process has a snowball effect. For months, you prepare yourself for a test, reviewing the content material assessed in the test. The scores that you earn indicates which courses you qualify to take. The ISAT scores can place you in advanced, honor or Advanced Placement (AP) classes in high school and the ACT scores can get you in the college of your dreams.

On the other hand, there are students who might say, "I do not want to be placed into any advanced or honor classes because those classes require too much work." In my opinion, students who think this way are slackers. They do not have a future planned out and do not aspire for much. They are satisfied with the minimum, whatever they can easily achieve. Personally, I do not want to be a person like that and I hope you do not either.

Knowing the purpose of the assessments you are taking is not the only skill that will allow you to score high. As Dr. Lourdes says, "Knowing how to take tests is a skill that all students need to master if they want to succeed in school and life." Knowing how to take tests involves managing your emotions. Your emotions, or the way you feel when you are taking a test, will have a huge impact on how well you do. A big reason why students score lower than expected on tests like the ACT is anxiety. Students let their emotions overcome them and they cannot think straight. It is understandable! I mean, you are taking a test that will more or less determine the course of your future. Who would not be nervous? The solution, although it may not be easy, is to learn to control your emotions and focus on what is important, the test. Anxiety, according to the National Library of Medicine, is a feeling of fear, unease, and worry, and can come from an event or thought that makes you feel frustrated, angry, or nervous. With the help of Dr. Lourdes and my co-writers, and I came up with my own definition of anxiety. Anxiety is the fear of failure! You might agree with my "definition" because it sounds very accurate. Right?

Most students get very nervous before any test, especially if the test is very important. They worry even more during the test, specifically when they start seeing the questions. It is also true that we get even more anxious once we start thinking that we will fail. You can control this anxiety and these nerves by knowing that you will not fail. Why? You should not worry when you know that you prepared yourself well; therefore, there is reason to be nervous. That is why I believe that more important than anything else is knowing what will be on these tests. If you know what the test is testing, then you can prepare accordingly. When you are prepared, there is no reason for you to be afraid. Some of my co-writers also suggested that thinking about happy things could help you fight test anxiety. Find "a place" in your mind where you can be happy or try any strategy that can help you relax your mind.

I also think that students should take advantage of any opportunity to improve their performance on the ACT. Since in the state of Illinois it is a requirement to take to the ACT in order to graduate high school, at my school there are many good opportunities to learn what is in the test and strategies to get the right answers. My school offers a lot of classes and assistance. In tenth grade, we also take the PLAN. The PLAN is very similar to the ACT. This is a good way to familiarized yourself, knowing what to expect when the real ACT comes along.

A couple months ago, I took a Saturday SAT prep-course. I did not know what to expect because I had never taken any SAT test nor practice. I did not know what the test was about or what to expect. It was a good opportunity though. I am glad I took it because it helped me improve my test-taking skills. That is why I strongly believe that good test-taking skills includes knowing what kind of test-items are on the test, knowing how many items will be in each section, and knowing how much time you have to complete each section of the test and the test as a whole. With much practice, I have drastically improved my ability to complete the test in the allotted time. I enrolled this year for an ACT study hall, which allows me, and my peers, to practice for the ACT and learn some strategies. The teacher that directs the study hall is an ACT expert and she gives us suggestions on what to do if we are stuck or do not know the answer. A good thing about the ACT is that there is no penalty for guessing, so if you are running out of time you can guess and increase your chances of choosing the right answer. During this ACT study hall, we also get to see the test questions that junior students failed to answer correctly (in their practice tests) and the correct answers. That way we can see and study the questions that students struggle the most so we can practice them more.

There are also ACT Prep classes offered on Saturdays. There are places that even offer ACT simulations! My school also offers the opportunity to take an ACT test at our school site apart from the National ACT testing day. Taking the ACT more than once is also a good way for improving your score because every time you retake the ACT you have a chance to improve your score.

According to Dr. Lourdes, "Mastering the content that will be assessed is as important as mastering the assessment process that will be used to assess the content." Mastering the assessment includes recognizing your strengths and weaknesses, practicing for the test, knowing what kind of test items will be in the test, and controlling your emotions. Doing all this will also require that you manage your time properly. How well you manage the time that you spend in test practices, studying for your classes, participating in school activities and dealing with family issues will make the difference between a well-prepared student and a student who does not know what to expect on a test. To be able to achieve your maximum level of academic proficiency, more than anything else you must focus on the goal of becoming the greatest test taker you can be. Although it might be scary to say, the truth is that your performance in tests will determine where life will take you. Are you up for the test?

Nicolas Barrios

EMBRACING YOURSELF

Every school day I walk through the crowded and very diverse hallways of West Aurora High School. I see the typical "popular people" yelling across the hall. I also see all of the other usual high school cliques - the "Goths", the "Weirdoes," and then those who struggle to fit in anywhere. I also see the ones who do not have many friends. In the past, I used to struggle making friends too. All that I lacked was someone to give me a little more self-confidence. It was not until now, my junior year, when I actually have an idea of who I am. I am, for the most part, comfortable with the student, neighbor, friend, brother, son, cousin, grandson, nephew, and overall person who I am.

In class, when I am bored, I usually look around the classroom. I can often easily tell who are comfortable with themselves and who lack self-confidence. I can determine their level of confidence by their posture, how often they raise their hand, and how loud they speak when the teachers ask them a question. Even the way you walk into a room can show your level of self-confidence. Some people walk right in like they own the place and others try to go unnoticed. Based on these acts, I can assume that some students are not comfortable with themselves. As Dr. Lourdes said, "Some of these students do not understand, accept, or appreciate who they are;" they simply do not embrace themselves. Yes! You need to embrace who you are so you can realize the brilliant person that stands on the other side of that mirror!

When you embrace yourself, you understand and know who you are. Often times, students do not recognize their own strengths and abilities. Students who do this only focus on their weak points, which eventually leads to negative feeling and an inability to do their tasks well. You can learn or figure out what you are good in by what your teachers and peers say about you, or the compliments you get in school. Take for example, one of my pre-calculus classmates always finishes the challenging problems first and usually gets them correct. The teacher compliments her every time she gets it right. The teacher excitedly says,

"Excellent!" My classmate is obviously strong in mathematics. I am sure she already knows that. Knowing what you are good at can help you choose your career. If you excel in biology, maybe you will find it interesting to earn a degree in biology.

Understanding yourself also helps you know how you learn best. Some students grasp things quicker than others do. At the same time, teachers will not slow down their teaching just because you failed a test. You cannot depend only on the teacher. That is why responsible students need to find new and different ways to study for a class or a test so they can excel in school. For example, too many hours completing your homework assignments could leave you with less hours to sleep. However, the amount of sleep you get either debilitates or benefits your learning and concentration throughout the school day. Another girl in my Physics class, who only gets two to three hours of sleep every night, always looks exhausted. She is never in a good mood! Although she is an outstanding student, I believe she must learn to manage her time better. She should know that her bad sleeping habits are affecting her as a person greatly. Therefore, no matter how difficult it might be, students must take time to get to know themselves.

Embracing yourself also requires that you accept who you are. We all have flaws and weaknesses. Not everybody likes to accept his or her own flaws and weaknesses, which may cause them to dislike themselves. Some people think they are too tall. For example, my friend always crouches down when he is standing up. Rather than trying to appear shorter, I think he should stand taller and look superior to everyone. Right? Other students think that they are too short for other people to notice them in school. Let me share with you a perfect example of a short person who truly embraces her short stature. In a room, in order for people to hear her, she will always speak louder than anyone else does. She will always find a way for students to notice and hear what she has to say.

The important thing about accepting your flaws is that you might be able to change what you realize you do not like. If you are overweight, first accept it and then try to lose weight. In addition, if you are a slow learner, rather than calling yourself stupid, accept it and put forth the extra effort you need to learn what you need to learn. Remember that there is no limit to what you can learn. The more effort you put into things the better they will turn out. If you are tall like my friend, use it to your advantage.

Get noticed! As my friend David said, "Everything you find wrong with yourself, find a way to turn it around." Dr. Lourdes shared with us how she sometimes feels sad about her weight gain. Then she stops to think and says, "I look pretty good for my age! My husband is a lucky man!" Some people find their cultural background embarrassing. Instead of neglecting or ignoring where you come from, learn more about it. You will be able to find the beauty or uniqueness and then use that knowledge to your advantage.

In many cases, people who do not accept who they are do not speak up because they feel people will only notice their flaws. These people are probably the brightest people in the room; however, they are unnoticed or ignored due to their lack of self-confidence. I used to be like that. I never raised my hand in class. After my teacher, Mr. Stern told us once that, "Doing things under pressure helps students learn better" and "If you get an answer wrong you will not explode," I started raising my hand a lot more. I sometimes realized how stupid my response to the question was after I heard the correct answer coming from another student. Can you guess what I did? I just brushed off the embarrassment and moved on! We cannot avoid failures; but we can always learn from them. Accepting and learning from failures requires choosing to be optimistic and willing to work harder. Your flaws are also part of who you are. Remember that things like salt and baking powder do not taste good by themselves, but when mixed altogether in a cake, the cake ends up tasting pretty darn delicious. When you embrace even your imperfections, you are able to move on and be more at ease with yourself. You will also learn to love yourself more.

As a student and as a person in general, you must appreciate who you are and what you have accomplished. Your accomplishments should be something you take pride in when you look back. Appreciate what you can do and do not let the things that you cannot do hold you back. Once you know your qualities, you will realize that not many people share them. You are unique! A friend of mine has won many soccer titles and has been doing great in his young soccer career. He often gets jealous though when he sees that in other countries, players of his age are playing in higher divisions. He always looks back to when he faced one of the best players of his age at the state level. He said, "If I beat him then I can beat anybody." Therefore, looking back at your accomplishments can motivate you to pursue even greater accomplishments, especially when things get tough. If you appreciate yourself, then you can definitely expect others to appreciate and respect you. I have a classmate in my pre-calculus who truly appreciates his ability to grasp the content. He will ask me, say, "Are you getting this?" As soon as I say that I am not getting it, he explains whatever I do not understand. Knowing that he understands the topic, gives him the confidence to go off and explain it to someone who does not understand as well as he does. This kind of self-confidence and willingness to help makes me and others appreciate his ability to understand calculus. He definitely earned my respect! Helping others also helps him feel good and proud himself.

You must also value how much hard work you have put into any task. For example, if your teacher mistakenly marks an answer wrong on your test, you can both ignore it and show that you could not care less about your grade, or you can go up and politely, but assertively, show the teacher the mistake he or she committed. Like my teacher Mr. Stern says, "You must self-advocate!" I believe that if you do that teachers will see that you are interested in doing well. Teachers might even like you more and be more careful the next time they grade students' assignments.

Appreciating yourself also has a lot to do with taking care of yourself. What you eat is very important. Your diet affects how you feel throughout the day. For example, my cousin Adriana is a health freak to the max! Whenever I see her, she seems to be in a great mood. She looks great! Over the course of the past three years, her body physically transformed. She realized that she did not like the way she looked; so she did all she could to change it. My P.E. teacher, Mrs. Proctor, always encourages us to exercise before we take our final tests in order the get "our brains going." Coincidentally, my academic mentor also exercises before he studies or does homework. I thought he was just a nerd who sat and studied all day.

In addition, people who dress nicely are likely to feel more confident. People who dress well are also the people who show they care about themselves. Subsequently, they catch other people's attention and never pass by unnoticed. My "buddy" Irving, for example, usually dresses more formal than most students do. He even walks with a little more strut. While walking in the hallway he always receives comments left and right, which makes him feel even better. However, the few rude comments that he sometimes get do not bother him. He is already so confident that he says,

"They're just jealous." Exercising, eating right, and dressing to impress not only can make you feel good but can also make you look better! Please, do not let laziness affect your physical appearance. Of course, occasionally we all have our "bumpy" days. Yet, they have a time and should be kept limited. To sum up, appreciating yourself and the things you have accomplished will help you embrace yourself.

To conclude, you must remember that nobody will ever love or understand you as much as you love and understand yourself. In the wild, when a lion from a pride is sick, the rest of the lions leave it alone. However, if a lion is healthy, all the others will accept him. Everybody wants to know and hang out with people who have positive attitude and take care of themselves. As Dr. Lourdes says, "People tend to like people who like themselves." In other words, embrace yourself. Embracing yourself consists of understanding, accepting, and appreciating who you are. Your self-confidence will open you doors. People will know you as a person who lightens up a day by simply saying hello.

Dr. Lourdes Ferrer

Rodolfo Lozano Jr.

BUILDING CHARACTER FOR SUCCESS

Many students have the ability to do great things but fail because they lack the drive to do so. I see this lack of motivation among all my peers, no matter their grade level, every day at West Aurora High School. Many students would like to achieve great things in their school career such as joining a sport team, starting an afterschool club, or running to be part of the Student Council; however, if they do not have respect for themselves or others, they will never be able to reach any of these goals. If students would just put forth the effort and stop relying so much on others to do things for them, then they would be able to achieve academic success and a superb quality of life. The pathway or road to this requires that students demonstrate the four character traits that are essential to academic and life success. These four character traits are responsibility, persistence, a strong work ethic, and the ability to delay gratification.

The first trait needed to achieve academic and life success is responsibility. One of the main reasons why being responsible is so important is that striving to become better requires that you are on top of most (if not all) of the things you are doing in your life. For example, it is my responsibility to maintain a good grade point average; but this requires that I manage my time wisely so I do not fall behind my schoolwork. Students who have the responsibility character trait embedded into their lives are able to follow anything through; that is, they do not leave things half way done. Responsible students are likely to enjoy their peer's trust and respect. Personally, I feel horrible when I forget doing things in my life that are moderately important, especially when I know that it was my responsibility to do them. I feel like people look down at me or lose their respect for me when I do not do what I am supposed to do. For example, not long ago I forgot to deliver an important package for my mother. Not doing so could have had major repercussions for my entire family and it made me realized how important it is to take responsibility for my own actions. On the other hand, always acting responsibly can help you achieve academic success. For example, if you do your assignments with integrity, and turn them in on time all the time, you will excel in all your classes and will not have any problem achieving academic success. You can also show responsibility by volunteering in your community. You will be not only helping others but also expanding your horizon, building connections and a good reputation with others. If you do things like that, I am sure that you will not have any problems reaching your goals throughout the rest of your life. This is why responsibility plays such a huge role in the ability for anyone to achieve academic and life success.

Another great way to achieve academic success and a quality life is by being very persistent when you are trying to accomplish your goals. Without persistence, and the drive to want to achieve that certain goal, you will not be able to do all the things you want to do in life. For example, if you really want to get an A in your math class but you do nothing to help you get that grade, then you are just saying words. There is no action behind your words. To get that A you will need to consistently say that you want that A and back up your words with properly using all the resources you have available including your book, class notes, classmates and the teacher. Persistence will help you achieve your goals because, even if you fail, you will get back up and try again. My experience as an athlete has helped me learn persistence. For example, when I was wrestling there were times that I lost matches after matches; nevertheless, my persistence helped me continue with my training and trying. With the support of my family and friends, I eventually became better at the sport and won my first wrestling match. Personally, I believe that without the drive and persistence to do something, you will accomplish very little in life. If you are not persistent, you will just slack for the rest of your life. Therefore, my advice to you is, "Get off your butt and try even if you fail!" In the end, persistence will help you see your dream come a reality.

To achieve academic success and a quality life you must have a strong work ethic. A strong work ethic requires that you put in the necessary effort, even when things get tough. You cannot give up! This kind of attitude will get you far. Colleges and jobs will want you there because you have consistently demonstrated great dedication in all you do in life. I know that when I really want something, I have to work hard to get it. For example, when I was a freshman in high school, I always wanted to get into the University of Iowa. Since this was my goal, I really buckled down and said to myself, "Rodolfo, you cannot goof around in school. If you really want this you will have to put a lot of work into your high school career." During all my years in high school, I kicked my own "rear" and studied very hard. I have accomplished my goal of getting good grades every year. When the time finally came to summit my college applications, I applied to the University of Iowa. I knew as a fact that I would continue to work hard in school even if I was not accepted into the school of my dreams. However, the big day finally came, the day I received a letter from the University of Iowa. That letter would say if I was accepted or not by the University of Iowa. I walked into my home and opened the letter. I was so nervous! I began to read the letter and then I jumped for joy because I got into the school of my dreams. This shows that hard work, persistence and responsibility can make your dreams come true.

The last thing you need to do to achieve academic success and a quality life is not to need immediate gratification. One of the reasons why we should wait, or not need immediate joy, is that even if we do something good now, we can always strive for something better. When you receive a good grade on the test, you should be happy but you should always try to strive for something better than that. For example, you should say to yourself, "I am happy that I got an A on the test, but I want an A in the class." If you have a part-time job and receive your paycheck, of course you will be happy that you earned that money. However, I am sure you would like to earn more than that. Right? You should not get too happy about that amount of money you are getting right now. On the contrary, you must strive for the knowledge and skills that will help you become a better person and receive a better job, and that is not now but later. When you delay your gratification, you recognize that there is plenty of room for personal improvement and you cannot just settle. You must always strive for greatness and that is not immediate. It requires time! The bottom line here is that most good things do not come or happen immediately. They require time and sacrifice.

In conclusion, I believe that we as students should strive for greatness. Not doing so will leave us "in the dust." We must have the internal drive to learn, grow and improve ourselves. Without that drive, we will be left behind. There will be people who want you to give up. You cannot listen to them. You must ignore them because they can drag you down with them. I know that if you demonstrate the four character traits that I wrote about, you may be fortunate enough to succeed academically as I did. Always remember to keep these traits in the back of your head at all times because they will help you throughout your life.

Dr. Lourdes Ferrer

DR. LOURDES' BIO

Growing up in a disadvantaged family in Puerto Rico, Lourdes soon learned that education was the way out of the poverty cycle. This understanding led her to complete her undergraduate degree in mathematics and begin teaching.

She left Puerto Rico in 1979 to do community development work in Guatemala. She established and directed schools, an orphanage, feeding centers, and clinics. She procured resources for these entities through interaction with non-profit organizations and by obtaining assistance from Guatemalan government officials. Her community education work consisted of educational radio programs and parent education in various venues. Her experience in community development was a catalyst that led Lourdes to choose Research, Evaluation, and Measurement as the focus of her Master's degree.

When she moved to the United States in 1990, she had to overcome enormous financial, linguistic, and cultural barriers to pursue the American Dream. She first worked as a Middle School Bilingual Curriculum Content (BCC) mathematics teacher in Dade County and then as Regular High School mathematics teacher in Palm Beach County.

She went on to complete her Doctoral Degree in Leadership and took a position as a School Improvement and Assessment Specialist for the School District of Palm Beach County. She was responsible for developing and implementing programs that assist schools in their school improvement efforts. These programs included staff development opportunities for teachers and school administrators, assessment literacy presentations as well as speaking at community forums regarding student academic achievement and performance gaps between diverse student populations.

In 2005, Dr. Lourdes left Florida to work as an Education Consultant in DuPage County, Illinois, and other school districts across the nation. Since then she has been analyzing student performance data and conducting qualitative studies to find out from the students', teachers' and parents' perspectives the reasons behind the lack of academic achievement of students on states' accountability tests. For the past eight years, she has developed numerous programs designed to increase the academic achievement of all students and close the stubborn academic achievement gaps between diverse student populations. These programs include state-approved academies for school administrators, staff development opportunities, student motivation presentations and parent empowerment seminars.

Dr. Lourdes' specializes in academic and non-academic issues regarding English Language Learners, Hispanic and African American students. She covers a wide range of topics that include cultural competency, achievement gaps between ethnic groups, parent empowerment, culturally relevant instruction, college and career readiness, math Common Core State Standards and state's accountability testing.

Dr. Lourdes is the author and facilitator of, Navigating the American Educational System (NAES) and In the Driver's Seat, two very popular and dynamic curricular and training programs, designed to help parents navigate the American Education System, monitor their children's education and ensure that their children receive a top-quality education.

She is also the author and facilitator of the Grooming for Excellence Student Leadership academy, a program designed to increase students' college and career readiness, motivate them to pursue STEM-related degrees and graduate college with the least amount of debts.

Dr. Lourdes is the author of the books Hispanic Parental Involvement: Ten Competencies Schools Must Teach Hispanic Parents, Siéntese en la Silla del Conductor: Las Diez Competencias Para Conducir a Sus Hijos al Triunfo Académico and the co-author of Voices: African American and Hispanic Students' Perceptions Regarding the Academic Achievement Gap. Her latest publications, Reactions: A Collection of Hispanic Student Essays and Reactions: A Collection of African American Student Essays are different from any other publication because she wrote them in collaboration with high school students.

DEBORAH'S BIO

Deborah Ferrer was born in Guatemala, Central America, a country also known as - the land of the eternal spring. In pursuit of a better life, at the age of four, her family migrated into the United States and established themselves in Florida. According to her mom, "During our first year, Deborah was the one who struggled the most. Going to school made her seriously ill. It made things very difficult for all of us."

After Deborah reached grade-level English proficiency and learned how to navigate the American culture, her mother enrolled her at U.B. Kinsey Elementary School of the Arts, one of the best elementary school in the county. At that early age, Deborah fell in love with the visual arts! She continued her pursuit of a highly specialized education in the arts throughout her middle school years. In 2000, she was admitted to the Alexander W. Dreyfoos School of the Arts, a nationally recognized high school in Palm Beach County. In her own word, "I literately battled to get myself accepted into that school. Hundreds of young artists auditioned and very few were accepted."

As a teenager, Deborah was determined to pursue a college career that required a strong foundation in the visual arts. To reach that goal she took advantage of every opportunity her high school offered. Besides meeting the school's visual arts requirements, she took all types of rigorous academic subjects. To earn some college credits, save some money and time, she enrolled and successfully passed the exams for AP Spanish and AP History.

Although Deborah was raised in home environment where the culture of learning prevailed, she knew that her mother, a single parent of three, was not in a position to cover all the costs of an out-of-state private university. She knew that to be accepted, and be able to finance her college education, she had to have a good GPA and a high ACT score. In her own words, "I was totally focused and I worked really hard!" In 2004, she graduated with a 4.5 GPA and an ACT score of 30. Her hard work paid off! She was one, of only 60 students nationwide, who received a 100,000-dollar scholarship to attend the Cooper Union School of Art, an elite university in New York City. Living in Florida at the time, this awesome news presented several challenges. She was a girl, the youngest of three children, and the first in the family to move thousands of miles away from home to pursue a degree in Fine Arts - something not common in the Hispanic culture.

Deborah soon fell in love with New York; and not long after that, she discovered the world of Architecture, a career that beautifully combines fine arts with applied mathematics. In 2006, she was accepted to the Irwin S. Chanin School of Architecture at the Cooper Union, a five-year degree program, and was the recipient of another 125,000 dollars in scholarships to cover her tuition.

Within those 5 years working towards her Architecture degree, she made another discovery – she had an innate passion for management and administration. She was hired by the Dean of the School of Architecture to manage the school computer studio. She worked as a manager for five years and her responsibilities included - supervising staff, meeting the students' computer needs, providing staff development and increasing the efficiency of the equipment.

In 2008, her sense of adventure, multicultural perspective and high academic performance got her into Ghana, Africa. She received a scholarship to study and build in a small under-developed village, a traditional adobe construction, using both new and old construction techniques. In spite of the challenges that an under-developed community presents, she successfully completed her work with the support of the villagers. Her likeability contracted the attention and love of the people.

In 2010, she earned another scholarship to travel to her home country of Guatemala to complete her college thesis. Her love for Guatemala, ability to communicate in Spanish and bold spirit opened wide doors to learn from Guatemalan engineers, architects and the community in general, the reasons behind the capital's sink holes. In spite of the government's opposition, she was able to get evidence that these 100 feet deep holes were created not solely by nature, but by leaking pipes of the sewer system, due to lack of maintenance, lax city zoning regulations and building codes. She earned the Cooper Union medal for Leadership and Excellence upon graduation in 2011.

Soon after graduating, she started working as a project manager for a construction firm in Orlando, Florida until 2012. During this year, she was able to see firsthand the strong connection that exists between civil engineers, architects and construction companies. She was able to experience the challenges of building homes that meet the clients' demands, within budgets and in accordance to the city's building codes. In her own words, "That year was worth a life of experience!"

Following her passion for business management, she put her architecture career aside, at least for a while, to accept a position as a Business Manager in a worldwide company specialized in exotic teas. Her responsibilities include hiring and training personnel, scheduling, doing payroll and most of all, meeting the company's financial goals for her ½-million dollar store. Since then, she has twice won a Certificate of Excellence and been recognized as one of the top ten General Managers in the company.

Ms. Ferrer also operates her own small business called Paper Cut, working as an art consultant, graphic and interior designer and book editor. She will soon be the co-author of the book, College Casualties: Twelve Competencies to Avoid Becoming One." This book, written for high school students (and their parents) provides readers with strategies to avoid dropping out of college, earning degrees that are not in demand or graduating with surmountable debts. Her goals right now are to - further develop her business skills, pursue a Project Management Certification and later on, earn a Master's in Material Science from MIT.

Dr. Lourdes Ferrer